This approach to understanding organisational cul[...]
I've found. Once you've seen the world this way, you c[...]
The book is an excellent introduction to a simple yet sophisticated
methodology for giving leaders agency to nurture and promote the sorts
of cultures we need in the organisations we lead.

Dyfed Alsop, Prif Weithredwr / Chief Executive, Awdurdod Cyllid
Cymru / Welsh Revenue Authority

I have always described culture as "what people around here do when
no-one is looking". It can therefore be difficult to read and to assess. Gill's
insights around the use of language and discourse provide incredibly
useful frameworks to codify culture for those involved in leading change.
Essential reading for those contemplating business transformation.

Paul Donovan, Serial CEO, Angel Investor and Venture Philanthropist

Easy to read and rich in ideas, this book will help you to understand how
the way we talk shapes the way we think, act and connect with each other.
The author combines her academic insights with practical experience to
offer ways to understand and shift the culture of your team, department
and organization and, most importantly, how to make it better for
everyone.

Kathryn Bishop CBE, Associate Fellow, Saïd Business School,
University of Oxford. Consultant and Non-Executive Director. Author
of *Board Talk: 18 crucial conversations that count inside and outside the
boardroom*

I was genuinely enthralled. I read it in two sittings and was delighted
to learn so much, even though I've worked with Gill. I remembered
how surprised we were to learn what her language work had revealed
about our culture. Macro conclusions from the analysis were not just eye
opening but actionable; the shock she mentions in the book was real and
was truly a catalyst for change.

Barb Agoglia, Founder of FreshEyes Business and Brand Strategy
Consultants, NYC. Former VP of Global Brand and Marketing for B2B
Payments, American Express

A must-read for anyone interested in organisational culture, in the
ongoing challenges of how to measure it, and how to change it. Gill Ereaut
provides a practical guide to understanding how a company's everyday
language can hold a mirror up to what people are really thinking and why

they are behaving as they do. If you want to transform any aspect of your organisation, you should read this powerful guide first.

Caroline Fawcett, Customer Experience Consultant and Non-Executive Director, Financial Services

For our Masters students in Organizational Psychology, Human Resource Management, and Management Consultancy & Organizational Change, this would be an inspiring and informative text, showing how a method that we introduce to them in an academic context (via methodological and empirical academic papers using discourse analysis) can also be used in organizational practice. In fact, many of our mature students already work in these fields and they would all potentially be interested in this book, even without their Masters student identities.

Gill Ereaut has done an amazing job in explaining and unpacking discourse analysis. The book includes some fantastic materials in the examples and case studies that really bring the discursive approach to life. It's a great read - I wish it had existed years ago when I started my own discourse analysis journey!

Rebecca Whiting PhD, Reader in Organization Studies at Birkbeck, University of London

A wonderful writing style - clear, unfussy, accessible, able to render complex ideas simply. It's a very rich distillation of decades of experience. The case studies/examples really made it come alive - these, and how the author uses them to illustrate specific language points, are a really important part of the book's uniqueness and readability.

Clare Anderson PhD, Bold Leap Consulting

In this interesting and accessible book, Gill Ereaut shows how language analysis can offer valuable insights into the self-organizing patterning of people's ongoing interactions that we think of as organizational culture. I recommend it to anyone who wants to gain a better understanding of how culture 'shows up' in the language used by people in their everyday conversations, and what this might mean for their own perspective, practice and performance.

Chris Rodgers, Director, Chris Rodgers Consulting Ltd. Author of *The Wiggly World of Organization* and *Informal Coalitions*

Organisations are usually judged using numbers like turnover or profits or return on investment. But this very important book explains how words are at least as important as numbers and indeed often more important, because language expresses and shapes culture, which is the most important determinant of organisational success.

Professor Sir Muir Gray, The Oxford Value and Stewardship
Programme

I've seen Gill's methods in action, and I know they work. She's now done us all a service by writing this clear and fascinating account of how she does it, and why the language people use every day makes such a difference to an organisation's performance.

Paul Feldwick, Author and Consultant

Gill Ereaut brings linguistic analysis into the boardroom and onto the shop floor and shows its power to clear the obstacles to cultural transformation in a wide range of businesses and public organisations. We all know that language matters: now there's a way to use this obvious insight to make a difference.

David Landsman OBE, NED, Chair and Adviser, Former Ambassador
and Executive Director

Gill Ereaut's unique approach is like structured alchemy - creating gold (a deep understanding of an organisation's culture) from the base metal of everyday language. Having experienced the work in practice, I can confidently say that anyone interested in or charged with nurturing a different organisational culture would do well to read this original, thoughtful and practical book.

Michael Coughlin, Public Sector Consultant and Transformation
Advisor to the UK Local Government Association

THE WAY WE
TALK
AROUND HERE

How your **organization's culture** shows
up in your **language**, and why it **matters**

GILL EREAUT

First published in Great Britain by Practical Inspiration Publishing, 2025

© Gill Ereaut, 2025

The moral rights of the author have been asserted

ISBN

      9781788605885 (hardback)
      9781788604840 (paperback)
      9781788604963 (epub)
      9781788604956 (Kindle)

Want to bulk-buy copies of this book for your team and colleagues? We can customize the content and co-brand *The Way We Talk Around Here* to suit your business's needs.

Please email info@practicalinspiration.com for more details.

Practical Inspiration
Publishing

Contents

Preface

Think back to your first few days in a new job, or to a time you joined an established group as a newcomer. Do you remember how it *felt*? And do you remember noticing the strange way people at the new place *talked*? If you're still part of that organization or group, can you *still* hear that language?

Typically, when you first join a new organization you can 'hear' its language – the weird way people there talk (and write). This is often true even if you arrived from another job within the same field or industry. You may feel disoriented, not just by the acronyms and the new words for old, familiar ideas, but by whole new ideas that are being named and discussed as if they're obvious. At the same time, other ideas and language – that had been 'obvious' and central to the discourse of your old place – are strangely missing. A disorienting time for anyone.

As a newcomer, you simply have to learn how to function in a new organization, to do the job you've been hired to do. So you just get on with it and work out what's going on, how to behave, who and what's important around here, and so on. Few people feel able to comment publicly on what they're experiencing at this time, because to do so could sound like criticism.

Then, a few weeks or months later, you can no longer hear the language. You've learned the jargon, yes, but more importantly you've absorbed the broader language and its *subtext* – the shared certainties that lie at the centre of the new culture. Joining a company, organization or other group means joining a 'discourse community' – learning its specific terms and abbreviations, but also the concepts, expectations and priorities of the group that are embedded in this language. In other words, its culture.

This creates a real difficulty for investigating organizational culture. The powerful norms of a culture are unspoken, and its assumptions are silent, and the only people who are aware of them are the new joiners – who are not usually in a position to comment. Once you're inside the organization and have learned how to perform your job within it, 'living' the culture necessarily becomes automatic and unconscious – it now just feels *normal*. And once you can no longer hear the peculiarities of the language as peculiar, you're no longer aware of what it's doing, and you can no longer fully grasp its implications.

How valuable would it be to help everyone in an organization return to that first-day-at-work state of awareness, although this time without the disorientation? That might allow everyone to access the unthinking, lived culture *consciously* again, in a way that would let everyone see the nature of what they're living in. Then perhaps you could all discuss what's going on and consider together its continuing usefulness.

That, in short, is the aim of the method for analysing organizational cultures that forms the substance of this book.

Origins and influences

The approach to organizational culture that I'll describe is a product of many influences and experiences across my life, and of a couple of personal idiosyncrasies. So, without sinking too far into autobiography, I hope that setting these out briefly will offer some context for what's to come.

Discovering etiquette books: what a revelation! For a few years as a child I spent every Saturday morning in our local public library, roaming the shelves for things to find out about. At 10 or 11 years old I was curious about so much. I felt, especially, that *I* didn't know what *other* people knew – those who seemed at ease, who knew who they were in the world and how it all worked. I guess I sensed that where there are hidden rules that you don't know, you're always at a disadvantage. Then one day I chanced upon the shelf of *etiquette* books – amazing! Here, helpful authors patiently spelled out the unspoken rules, norms and assumptions that you needed to understand if you were going to fit in. Never mind that in reality I was never going to turn up at a Buckingham Palace garden party, nor be obliged to pour tea for a bishop – the idea that powerful but unspoken rules of behaviour could be *articulated* struck me as wonderful and, in fact, liberating. You'll see as we go on how those ideas, and the emancipation that comes with being able to see the invisible and hear the unspoken, has driven much of what I've done professionally since.

Qualitative market research: learning to listen. My early career was in commercial qualitative market research in the UK. I spent many years interviewing consumers and others in order to help organizations understand their customers, develop new products and work out what was going on when they had problems with products and services. This work taught me the discipline of qualitative data sampling and how to do thorough and systematic qualitative analysis. More importantly, through many years facilitating unstructured interviews and group discussions, I came to see how valuable it is to *listen* to people and really hear what they're saying – not just the 'content' but the social and cultural import of what they're saying, and of the way they're saying it.

'Planet Client': a strange and fascinating world. Through that market research practice, I came into regular contact with teams in organizations who were commissioning and using the work we did. I always found interviewing customers, citizens, patients, etc. stimulating, but over time I became increasingly interested in how the people in my *client* organizations talked.

Sitting, for example, in a briefing meeting in a 20th-floor conference room in a shiny building in some city, I'd listen to a group of marketers and others explain the issue or opportunity they had, and describe the lives, motives and needs of their customers. The shared language of these meetings seemed to sustain a powerful internal mental world – one populated by clear concepts, cemented by common terms, and with 'obvious' logical links that for those teams had a solid reality and truth. I began to think of this as 'Planet Client' – a rather interesting alien world with its own version of reality. However, that planet very often proved to be at odds in important ways with the planet inhabited by their customers when I met them. It wasn't that those customers used different words for the same things, but that they carved the world up into quite different concepts and categories, and made their own unique leaps of logic. They had their own version of reality. It was my job to translate between these worlds and it was interesting and challenging work.

Later, when those client teams were presented with the research findings, they'd invariably welcome the new and sometimes radically different perspective on customers' lives they'd gained. But it was astonishingly easy for them to lose their grip on that perspective. From the outside, it often looked like their subsequent decisions and actions ran counter to the customer insight they'd obviously grasped and valued at the time. It was as if the new information they received had quickly snapped back to the grid provided by their existing assumptions and narratives. A few years on from the original project (since the problem or opportunity hadn't gone away) they'd request essentially the same work, for a second or even third time.

This seemed highly wasteful – but as a puzzle to be understood, it was fascinating. Why did it seem so hard for people in organizations to break out of engrained mental models for long enough to take in, hold, process and use new information from the outside? I didn't have a way to get hold of this then, but I sensed that language was in some way implicated.

Discourse analysis: the answer I needed. At the time that I was in those briefing meetings and first noticing the apparently concrete effects of an organization's shared language, I had no way to conceptualize that effect, nor to work with it. I had become familiar with semiotic analysis, which allows cultural interpretation of visual signs and symbols, but then I discovered discourse analysis – a range of academic and applied research methods for looking closely at language and what it does. And this was exactly the conceptual and practical tool I needed.

This led me to form a specialist research and consulting company – Linguistic Landscapes Ltd – in 2002. I wanted to see if I could adapt discourse analysis approaches from academia to help organizations become more aware of the potential effect of their internal language, and how it's connected with their thinking, and help reduce the waste that could easily flow from that. Much of the content of this book, and the examples in it, unsurprisingly come from projects carried out for clients of Linguistic Landscapes and from the conversations, ideas, experiments and experiences co-created with colleagues, clients and collaborators across the past 20 years.

Edgar Schein's model of culture: just the right framework. Around the time I founded the company, I was introduced to the work of organizational culture expert and practitioner Edgar Schein, and to his early model of culture (2004). He described the differences between what's visible on the surface of an organization (what he terms 'artifacts'), the values and ideas that its leadership claims ('espoused beliefs and values') and the silent assumptions and taken-for-granted assumptions that lurk beneath ('basic underlying assumptions'). His model offered me a vocabulary to begin to explore the particular role of language as an artifact. This has been a crucial influence on what you'll read about here, and there's more about Schein in Chapter 2.

Complexity: from flocking birds to changing conversations. A few years later I began to work with a group of people who were using 'complex adaptive systems' as a conceptual framework to help resolve problems in large-scale organizations, such as the UK's National Health Service. What does that mean? You may be familiar with the computer simulations of the 1990s that managed to replicate the way that very large groups of birds 'flock' – swooping in the sky together in highly coordinated but unpredictable patterns. The computer birds (known as 'boids') could be shown to display rather realistic-looking flocking behaviour by each independently implementing just three simple rules, concerning keeping distance from neighbours and broadly how to choose a direction in which to head (see Reynolds 1987).

With this model as a metaphor, I started to think of the underpinnings of cultural behaviour (people in an organization metaphorically 'flocking') as akin to those simple rules, and to use discourse analysis of people's language to bring to the surface ideas about what these rules might be. This has proved to be a powerful metaphor and has helped many clients reformulate what they mean by 'culture' and especially by 'changing the culture.'

More recently a different development of complexity within organizational studies has also come into sight for me. 'Complex responsive processes' (Stacey 2001) combines ideas of complexity originating in the natural sciences with a range of ideas and models drawn from the social sciences, in order to take into account the extreme variability of humans when they interact. Those computer 'boids' were identical and were following the same simple rules. This is clearly not true of people in organizations – there may be coordination, but there will also be inconsistency. Humans are highly variable and are not good at following simple rules, even when they think they're doing so.

It makes sense to me that meaningful change in an organization involves in some way *changing the ongoing conversations* between people at all levels (Shaw 2002). Culturally shaped interaction, spoken or written, is the everyday working medium of an organization, and it seems obvious that change might best come about through the same medium.

Clients, colleagues and collaborators: trust, experimentation and shared learning. In 2002 I began in earnest to develop the methods that I'll describe in this book. Throughout that process I gained immeasurably from the many people – clients, colleagues, collaborators, associates and others – who were willing to trust, experiment and learn together to develop the approach and its capabilities. And I'm hugely grateful for and humbled by that trust and shared work, which still continues.

Along the way I've also worked alongside and benefited from the thinking of experts in other specialized frameworks and methods, including appreciative inquiry, semiotic analysis, quantitative research, natural language processing, behavioural science and more.

With the invaluable help of all these people, the Linguistic Landscapes business has thrived for more than 20 years, carrying out hundreds of research and consulting projects for large organizations in the public, private and third sectors in the UK, USA, Canada and Australia.

My aims for this book

What can you expect to get from this book? My main motivation in writing it has been to share the learning that, with colleagues, I've accrued over the last two decades about language and organizational culture, and to invite you to be curious about its possibilities for your own organization.

This book is particularly for people who are open to the idea that language is a powerful but unacknowledged force within organizations, and who are curious about its effects and its potential. I've met many such people within organizations – those who have an intuitive sense that language *matters*. If you're one of these, you might, for example, feel that your organization's internal language is odd or dysfunctional, or you suspect that it creates barriers; you may also be able to point to individual examples of such language. However, you find you can't fully develop and use your intuitions because you don't have a way to investigate, codify and apply the insights arising from them. This is the gap I aim to address with this book.

I want to show how everyday language in your organization offers a potent set of clues about what sits beneath its surface – which we might term 'culture'. The way people talk and write in your organization, about anything and to anyone – internal and external, formal and informal, virtual or in real life, in a board presentation or at the water cooler – can point to the unspoken ideas and tacit assumptions that silently reflect, shape and sustain how you collectively think, interact and operate.

I'll share some of the methods and tactics that I and colleagues have developed over the past decades for using language analysis to shine a light on culture, reflecting it back to the people whose working lives it moulds and whose customers it affects. And how to use those insights with them to provoke productive conversations across the organization. I'll also show the steps our clients have taken to begin to evolve their culture and keep adjusting it for current needs – and, in fact, to keep it permanently in view.

My intention is to make a language analysis 'mindset', and some basic methods, available to people without technical linguistic skills. There are certainly specialist linguistic/discourse consultants who can help you, but there's much you can do yourself to spot cultural clues in organizational language and perhaps to engage productively with them. Language plays a central role in maintaining your collective set of cultural assumptions and norms. If you can become attuned to this, and help others become equally sensitive, you'll have a useful understanding of what you mean by your culture. You might also have a shared vocabulary for discussing what's working in it, what's not working and how you might together change your organization for the better.

Very few members of staff, managers or even leaders have the remit to change *everything* affecting organizational culture (if such a thing were even possible), but that doesn't mean that nothing can change. You can affect, by your own actions, some of what goes on in your area, function, directorate or team; and you can certainly work to reshape your own interactions with those others whose perceptions and habits have an impact on your own work.

A note about examples and case studies

It's best to explain and illustrate concepts with examples and case studies, and I've accumulated a lot of these. However, by definition, most organizations seeking help with their culture have found themselves in a bad or difficult place and are not over-keen to publicize these details widely, even after the event. In addition, some of the work described here is fresh and ongoing. So, all the examples have been anonymized and/ or key details changed. I hope you will, nevertheless, find them helpful – they're all derived from real situations, issues and projects.

It's worth noting that the majority of our culture projects have been commissioned to help long-established businesses and organizations address challenges with their culture. So, much of what I'll cover illustrates how cultures can become stuck and indeed do damage to and impede organizational success, however that's defined. So I'm afraid at times the cumulative effect of the examples might feel a little negative.

However, the principles of understanding, tracking and course-correcting this crucial element of an organization have equal relevance in newer, emerging organizations. In fact it can be even more powerful – starting off well and keeping an embryonic culture healthy with constant attention is a wise leadership and management strategy for growing organizations. There are two examples of this kind of project at the end of the book, in Chapter 10, where I cover the idea of culture as a constant, conscious and positive conversation.

For users of languages other than English

The linguistic analysis examples described in this book are primarily derived from, and illustrated by, our work in English with clients in the UK, USA, Canada and Australia, and in international or global organizations using English as a lingua franca.

If you're working in a language other than English, you may find that a particular linguistic idea or category that I'm using doesn't exist in your language, or that it exists but is expressed differently. I hope nevertheless that these examples offer useful guidance and inspiration for your own exploration of language and its connection with your own, lived organizational culture.

Gill Ereaut
2024

Introduction

What is organizational culture anyway?

I need to clarify what I mean by organizational culture. For something held to be so important, it can prove slippery and hard to define.

The dominant way of speaking about organizational culture today presents it as a thing, like any business asset, that can be managed, controlled and changed. It's acknowledged to be hard to change culture, but efforts are nonetheless made to 'measure' and 'fix' or 'set' the culture; these tasks are often tackled by external consultants and consulting companies who are outside the organization. Measurement and description using dimensions and statistical norms developed from large data sets may then lead to a definition of the 'ideal' culture and to culture change programmes of various kinds. This way of solidifying culture and seeing it as something that exists outside the messy world of human beings, and the human interactions by which the organization operates, is naturally attractive within a business and organizational discourse. The idea of 'delivering' a new culture to solve organizational problems, or 'fixing' a 'broken' culture by persuading staff to think and behave differently, understandably has great appeal to organizational leaders. However, solid consistent evidence of its usefulness as a way to work with and change culture seems lacking.

I've found it more helpful to work with a different conceptualization of culture, captured in the rather vague but ubiquitous phrase: *'The way we do things around here'*. Many original sources are credited with coining this phrase, but it was certainly used early on by Deal and Kennedy (1982 p. 4), who themselves adapted it from Bower (1966). What matters for my purposes is how common it is – it's clear that for many, it's a highly meaningful way to refer to their own experience of organizational culture.

That phrase seems to capture an idea that culture is a set of learned, habitual behavioural and interactional norms, underpinned by a shared set of assumptions. To operate within an organization means to work within an ongoing set of taken-for-granted ideas and implicit norms, and generally (once past the first few weeks in the job) it means using those ideas unconsciously and automatically.

By this definition then, *everything is cultural*: the micro-choices people make in day-to-day operations; the way problems and opportunities are handled, and how they're defined as problems or opportunities in the first place; and how new information is made sense of and evaluated. Cultural fingerprints are on how people interact, conversations that happen (and those that don't), how decisions get made, what counts as knowledge and how it gets shared (or not), what counts as important, how tightly people hang on to what's familiar, how cohesive or fragmented groups are within the organization – and much more. It's the 'operating system' underpinning everything that's done and decided. It contains traces of the organization's history and it's the informal milieu in which newcomers find themselves.

Culture is best seen as a *practice*. We don't *have* an organizational culture, we collectively *do* our culture, enacting, reinforcing and recreating it every day. Quite literally, it's 'the *way* we *do things* around here' – a description of *the manner in which activity happen*s, not a thing or a noun. Importantly, for questions of change, this means that culture as a process (culture being *done*) can be dynamic and fluid and perhaps open to negotiation, while culture as a noun (culture being a *thing* that the organization *has*) carries connotations of being fixed and unchanging, at least without the application of some intervention from outside.

My work with colleagues, clients and partners over the past 20 years has led to three 'culture questions', and these provide a structure for much of my later content. The questions capture elements of culture that are particularly elusive but that we've seen in play when an organization seeks help with its culture because of internal issues and/or issues with external stakeholders such as customers.

These culture questions are:

- ▶ **Who are 'we' and what really matters around here?**

- ▶ **Who do we assume 'they' are out there (customers, competitors, regulators, students, patients, partner organizations and more), and what do we think of them?**

- ▶ **How do we 'do' relationships around here – with each other and with 'them' out there?**

You might say that the public mission/vision/values statements of any decent organization should answer these questions and provide guidance for staff about 'how to do things around here.' However, it's rare for culture as *described* and culture as *lived* to be identical or, possibly, even similar. Culture as lived is best thought of as a set of unspoken, tacit and implied norms and assumptions about how people should behave and interact that may bear little resemblance to the official position, but that affect every action and shape every decision.

It's probably a measure of how well the 'way we do things around here' phrase chimes with people's lived experience that it appears again and again. And, of course, that's why I borrowed and adapted it for the title of this book.

However, in adapting it, I want to emphasize that 'the way we talk' – the day-to-day language used in meetings, conversations, documents and so on – is not only part of 'the way we do things' but has a powerful and valuable role in its own right in giving access to what we think of as culture. That is, language has particular qualities that make it a powerful lens through which to examine organizational culture. I'll say more about these properties in Chapter 3.

A linguistic approach to uncovering culture: 'discourse analysis'

Before going any further, I'll give a quick introduction to the linguistic methods I use, which together are known as 'discourse analysis.' There will of course be much more on these methods later, especially in Chapter 3.

I'm using an umbrella term 'discourse analysis' to refer to a wide range of academic thinking and research methods, whose core ideas arose over the past four decades, emerging almost simultaneously in academia across various social sciences, linguistics, history, political studies, philosophy and literary criticism.

'Discourse analysis' as a whole contains many methods but some key ideas. These include the notion that language isn't a transparent and neutral medium for transmitting ideas about a fixed reality, but that it itself *constructs* that reality. Talk isn't *opposed* to action but *is* action. Language does things and specific language choices (words, grammar and much more) do those things in a particular way.

So, for our purpose in investigating organizational culture, 'the way we *talk* around here' is a significant part of 'how we *do things* around here.' An example will help to show this way of thinking. Below are fragments of different customer complaints to an airline, data from a project to look at how the organizational culture affected the way they handled such complaints, and to help them improve that. An important question for any discourse analysis is: what's being *done* with or *achieved by* this language? What identities are being created or sustained, relationships enacted or disrupted, power asserted or conceded and so on?

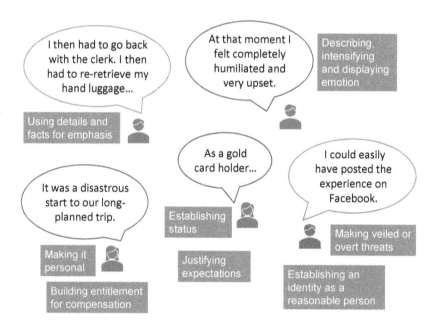

These fragments show various ways in which different customers introduced or described their complaint. If we see this language as *doing* something, we can begin to imagine what these language choices were designed to do, even if unconsciously.

- One statement works to establish the customer's status and perhaps prepare the ground for a claim to favourable treatment (*As a gold card holder…*).

- Another works to build up an identity as a 'reasonable' person, albeit one capable of making a veiled threat (*I could easily have posted the experience on Facebook*).

- A third uses intensified language to underline the negative emotional effect of the incident (*At that moment I felt completely humiliated and very upset*).

- Another builds up the personal significance of the ruined trip, perhaps working up a moral entitlement to compensation (*…our long-planned trip*).

- And the last one narrates at length (this is a fragment) every last detail of the incident, drawing attention to the length and tediousness of the experience (*I then had to go back with the clerk. I then had to re-retrieve my hand luggage…*).

It doesn't matter how consciously any of this action was carried out. What matters is the interactive work that those choices appear to perform – what they arguably 'invite' the agent to think, feel and say in response. This is language as action.

Significantly, discourse analytic methods are often used to study politics and power – that is, how existing relationships and distribution of resources can be made to seem 'unremarkable' and 'natural' through the way they're talked or written about. It's the way that ideas embedded in habitual, everyday language develop an 'unremarkable' and 'natural' quality that makes analysing discourse so valuable in excavating the unquestioned conventions and unspoken norms of an organization. Analysing the everyday language shared within a group will point to what's being taken for granted and *not* said. It suggests the frames of reference, ideas and beliefs – about ourselves, others and our relationships – that are unspoken but that must be there in order for that language to make sense.

'Discourses' offer frameworks for inference and judgements – about what things mean, what's right and what's wrong, what's acceptable and not acceptable, and what flows logically from what. It's important to note that 'discourses' are culturally and historically specific, and over time the social realities and meanings they sustain may shift. Language has the power to keep things the same in ways that are not always obvious, in that it's hard to think about or promote ideas for which there's no shared language. New language can, in contrast, channel such ideas and give them solidity and perhaps legitimacy. We see this when a phrase suddenly captures something that's perhaps been felt but has been hard to talk or think about. For example:

> ▶ In the 1999 MacPherson report on the UK Metropolitan Police's handling of the investigation of the murder of black teenager Stephen Lawrence in 1993, the official report used the phrase 'institutional racism' many times and this phrase immediately became a lightning rod for ideas, discussion and action. Used to describe racism at a structural or institutional level, rather than the racist behaviour of individuals, that term had in fact been around since the 1960s, but its use in the report brought it huge prominence in the UK. Arguably, it was then widely available within public discourse to crystallize experiences, practices and feelings that had been present before in the UK, but that had lacked a language and thus legitimacy and focus.

Language has material *consequences* (as those involved in 'spin' are very aware), and habitual language can make certain things appear inevitable, possible or impossible. Internal language landscapes can thus facilitate, or block, a company's ability to do important things such as grasp alternative directions or solutions, or to connect effectively with external groups. The power of language is not lost on those interested in making the resources of organizations and wider society more open to all people, regardless of background – language is, of course, a key part of the discussions about diversity, equality and inclusion taking place in many organizations.

Shared, familiar internal language keeps organizational culture relatively stable and constant. If everyone is using certain forms of language, yet no one can see them enough to evaluate their implications, the shared discourse just carries on doing the work it's doing. Gaining some awareness of the hidden role of language, and thinking about what ideas it might be perpetuating, is a positive first step towards evaluating and perhaps changing those ideas.

Looking at language through the lenses I've described in this book also offers a powerful way to do things *other* than change or evolve a culture. Here are three ways in which I and colleagues have applied this thinking in commercial consulting for private, public and third-sector organizations:

- **Culture:** Analysing the internal language of an organization to suggest its unspoken assumptions, for the purpose of understanding and perhaps helping those inside to understand and evolve that culture or address particular issues that appear to arise from it. *This is the primary focus of this book.*

- **Customers:** Analysing the language of customers and other stakeholders, to suggest the assumptions and world view that they might share on specific issues. Often comparing that with language used by an organization or team in order to understand any disconnects and to allow the organization to 'hear', address and interact with those customers and stakeholders better.

- **Context:** An analysis of the external discourse context for an organization is a valuable exercise – how objects and social constructs that are of interest to the aims of the organization, such as 'disability' or what 'a home' means, are constructed more broadly in the world (in media, social media, cultural artifacts such as books, films, cartoons and so on). This forms the context within which items such as communications, new products or campaigns will be understood and evaluated, so such insight is helpful to develop strategy, communications and marketing of all kinds. It's especially helpful when an organization wishes to disrupt or redefine that broader context; for example, in challenging and redefining what 'disability' means in public discourse.

It's beyond the scope of this book to go into the last two areas in detail, but, as we go, I'll show a few examples of work where internal discourse has crept across the boundary and affected interactions with others in that broader discourse context.

Why think about culture, and why now?

Today it's hard to avoid the idea of organizational culture; a quick look online at books and articles about organizations, leadership and management of all kinds will testify to this. 'Organizations' here can, of course, include commercial enterprises but also government and public sector bodies, schools and universities, charities, non-governmental organizations (NGOs) and other not-for-profit groups.

Culture within organizations has become a hot topic for discussion in the business world and far more widely:

▶ It's now common to regard organizational culture as crucial to organizational success – famously captured in the now rather overused headline: 'Culture eats strategy for breakfast', a phrase often attributed to Peter Drucker but of contested origin.[1]

▶ 'Culture' features openly in how organizations attract, recruit and retain talented people – and in how people choose companies to work for.

▶ Business startups describe and proudly celebrate what they see to be their cultures.

▶ No corporate website is complete without a statement of 'our culture'.

▶ It has become known that, in certain organizations, dubious or toxic practices have been normalized, such that behaviour that would never be sanctioned outside its boundaries is tolerated or even celebrated. This is often described as a 'culture problem' or as a 'toxic' culture.

▶ Lastly, organizational cultures are becoming the focus of hard regulation. For example, UK regulatory bodies such as the Financial Conduct Authority are taking an interest in how corporate and board cultures affect decisions and practices in organizations. They're seeing 'the tone at the top' as a part of what they need to assure and regulate, especially since the 2008 financial crisis.

So, it seems, belief in the real, concrete effects of an organization's culture is widespread, and culture is no longer regarded – as it once was – as 'the soft stuff' or as a 'nice to have'.

There are plenty of reasons to pay attention to organizational culture in general. More specifically, here are a few comments I've heard from individuals seeking our consulting help for specific situations, from across a wide range of sectors. Do any of these resonate with you?

'I'm leading a major strategic change and I know it means people will need to change how they think and behave. And I know that won't be easy.'

'Culture feels like it's an issue for us at a whole-organization level, but within that I'm trying to help my team thrive. I can't fix the whole thing.'

---

[1] https://quoteinvestigator.com/2017/05/23/culture-eats/

'I'm facing a clear and present risk posed by a "toxic" culture – I'm an insider seeing actions I don't like.'

'I've been appointed as someone responsible for changing an outdated/ unhelpful/stuck/fragmented culture.'

'I have a suspicion that our culture is not helping this organization. And there's something odd about our language that adds to that feeling and my unease.'

'The way we talk around here doesn't seem to reflect the kind of organization we say we are or want to be.'

The last two statements clearly connect directly with the focus of this book – where someone already has that sense that language might be involved in some way with culture. However, the process of using internal language to shed light on culture doesn't need to start with identification of language as an issue, nor end in language recommendations. This approach has proved to be versatile. For example, we've carried out research and consulting projects to uncover an organizational culture where the larger aim was to:

▹ Evolve a faltering culture to bring it up to date for current circumstances or adapt to immediate environmental and other disruption – a remedial process.

▹ Evolve an established culture to support planned strategic or operational change.

▹ Use cultural insight to improve the interface between the organization and external groups such as users, customers, etc., or some other specific external group, using it to inform a range of activities (not just language).

▹ Build a coherent culture after a merger or acquisition – for example, when an organization with an extremely egalitarian culture acquires one with an extremely hierarchical culture.

▹ Improve or build a team culture – applying the same principles with a team to understand how that team could work best, even within an organizational culture that may feel problematic or alien.

> ▸ Nurture a successful embryonic culture, helping it to weather expected or planned change – for example, as the organization grows.

The last one has been in response to this kind of request that we've had from time to time:

'I'm proud of our culture and want to make sure it lives on as we grow bigger.'

In the final chapter I'll show a couple of examples where we've worked with new organizations to help sustain and gently evolve an already successful culture as the organization grows. (See 'When startups grow up' in Chapter 10.)

SECTION I:
WHY THE WAY WE TALK AROUND HERE MATTERS

In this section I'll set out a few conceptualizations of organizational culture and explain my practice-based theory about how cultures work, how they become stuck or dysfunctional, and how everyday internal language offers a useful proxy for analysing and working with culture. I'll also develop the three big cultural questions emerging from this practice that I mentioned in the Introduction, and that give structure to the linguistic content of the rest of the book.

Chapter 1
The public and private faces of organizational culture

The insider's typical perspective on their workplace culture is held within the apparent surrender of the phrase 'the way we do things around here', and especially its common rendering as 'it's *just* the way we do things..', as if it defies explanation. As an astute colleague dryly commented, this phrase is the linguistic equivalent of a shrug.

However, making implicit cultures explicit may be essential for organizations' health and success, as they attempt to keep up with social, political, economic and other change. Organizational culture is also no longer clearly entirely a private matter, since the consequences of a toxic or amoral culture have repercussions for many innocent outsiders and employees.

So how can people better see and think about the organizational cultures within which they work?

When organizational culture becomes public

First, we'll look at how a particular organizational culture typically becomes visible beyond the organization's walls. There are a few ways:

- ▶ *The declaration*: Many organizations make a public statement about 'our culture'. An overt statement of 'our culture' is commonly conflated with 'our values' and/or 'our purpose', also publicly stated. So the webpage headline is: 'Our culture and values' or 'Our purpose and culture' or 'Our purpose, values and culture', or one of many other permutations. As a language analyst, I'm always interested in exactly how these are stated. They're often a set of abstract words, a tumbling mix of nouns, adjectives and adverbs: Integrity, Excellence, Together, Sustainable, Respect, Caring and so on. Despite this abstraction, the entity in question is very clearly being presented as a 'thing', with a concrete reality to it.

Early on in a company's life, codifying the way people are working together as 'our culture' can record and celebrate the founder's philosophy, and capture that which is seen to have made/be making the young company successful. In mature organizations, a culture declaration *can* record and celebrate success in the same way, but may in fact represent a wish or aspiration.

A declared culture *may* reflect something of the 'lived' culture, but often it doesn't – it's not unusual for employees to laugh when they read their own company's public descriptions of culture and values. So a corporate statement about 'our culture' that's clearly divorced from the lived reality of those inside can represent an attempt to 'fix' the culture, when leadership believe it to be outdated or faulty.

▶ *The insider track*: Platforms such as Glassdoor are now trying to make lived internal cultures visible to outsiders. (Glassdoor is an online space where employees post information about their experience of working for a particular organization, often in answer to questions from those applying there for a job.) People seeking work – and not just the young ones – increasingly care about the culture of their workplace, and before they sign up they want early access to the culture that's lived and felt, not what's claimed or advertised.

▶ *The exposé*: An organizational culture may be dragged into public view through a scandal. So-called toxic cultures accommodate behaviour that would be seen outside the organizational bubble as immoral, unethical, reckless or even illegal. This behaviour is allowed, or even treated as normal, by most insiders. Eventually – possibly after many years – the hidden toxic cultural norms may be revealed when that behaviour is exposed, and it becomes clear to outsiders that something is terribly wrong. In the UK in recent years we've seen several such exposés, including the cultures of the Metropolitan Police, the Post Office and a significant NHS hospital trust.

The consequences of certain cultural norms can be material and serious – the Post Office scandal put innocent people in jail and financially ruined countless others; the NHS trust case resulted in the unnecessary death of several hundred people. Other cultural exposés, such as Enron, Sackler and Greensill, are well-known examples from the private sector.

▶ *Culture 'leakage'*: Even without deliberate sharing or exposure of a lived culture, it's common for organizational cultures to show themselves in what I've come to refer to as 'leakage' to the outside world. Such leakage is felt by people who come into contact with the organization, and it has consequences; for example, the ability to attract and connect with customers or users and to keep them happy, or to recruit the best talent.

So despite a company's overt claims about 'putting customers first', for example, it may be clear to customers from their interactions with that organization that they're far from 'first'. Cultural norms communicate themselves to outsiders and newcomers as a *feeling*, a sense of what and who does and doesn't matter within an organization, and what its people collectively think of groups outside.

Internal attitudes and assumptions 'leak' into external communications and conversations, not through the use of specific terms (although this does happen) but through far subtler means. These attitudes – 'this is what we think of ourselves, and of you' – are highly likely to make their way into language choices as well as into decisions about priorities, structures and a range of organizational activities.

For example, one of our client organizations, where a certain inflated pride was a cultural norm, consistently produced marketing materials that began with a lengthy fanfare about the company itself (not the reader or customer). Something like: '*At Company xxx, we always strive to create great products… so that's why we've spent months coming up with… and now we want to announce the launch of our new….'* The text reached line 10 or 15 before there was any mention at all of 'you', the customer. Until our analysis showed the teams how this was replicated as a pattern, they were completely unaware of it, and unaware of the effect it might be having on the reader.

It's also not uncommon for organizations to use slang or shorthand ways of referring to outsider groups that are suboptimal or even downright dismissive – see Chapter 6. Attitudes embedded in this internal language are likely to be 'felt' by those same people; not through the use of overtly dismissive language, of course, but because that mindset can make its way past the filters of even the best marketing and PR.

Persistent problems in connecting with users, attracting talented people from diverse backgrounds or addressing particular customer groups may reflect an internal culture that's unconsciously unwelcoming or alienating to those people. Cultures also leak out to important others, such as regulators and investors, and to talented people you might want to recruit and retain. Culture works all the time, even when no one is watching it.

Culture as experienced within the organization

Many employees agree that culture is what they *experience* and what happens in *practice* – only rarely the same as what's written down. Most often, cultures operate in barely noticeable ways, in the lived experience of everyday talk and action – it's *just* 'the way we do things here'. Again, notice the 'just' – culture is 'just' everyday practice. As the old saying goes, the fish swimming in the ocean doesn't notice the water.

Culture is the sum effect and enactment of unwritten norms and unspoken assumptions. It's not what's dictated from above but is made and sustained every day, by everyone – and it comes down to simple shared beliefs, habits and rules of thumb. For most of the organizations we worked with, there were perhaps five to seven key ideas at the heart of how people operated at that time.

As I mentioned in the Preface, early research into complexity in the natural sciences showed that a few simple 'rules' can account for the spectacular collective movements of flocking birds. It's unlikely that, once humans are involved, the picture is that simple, but the general principles that mass behaviour is an emergent product of individuals acting and interacting is a useful way to think about highly complex, coordinated behaviour within organizations, and therefore about what 'culture' might be.

To me, this helps explain why cultures are so hard to change. Shared habits and norms offer cognitive shortcuts and reduce mental load in ever-more-pressured work environments. They're also familiar and, as such, may be comforting, and they reduce personal risk; people effectively develop an inner voice that says, 'If in doubt, do this/prioritize this/ignore this'.

I should mention here the role of leaders, sometimes described as 'setting the culture' or that 'it comes from the top'. Leaders have undoubted influence, but I believe that the gravitational pull of an existing culture, supported by its tendency to drop below visibility for those involved, makes it a black hole that pulls everything into its centre. So, as a leader or senior team, you can't just decide where the culture needs to go, announce it and expect a change. It's not a concrete asset to be manipulated and changed by the imposition of an order, or even a campaign of persuasion.

However, this is not to say that trying to *lead* change is futile – what's essential is for leaders to have and communicate a meaningful vision, and to publicly commit to and model appropriate everyday cultural behaviours, including language, that support that vision.

How cultures fossilize and why it matters

We need to consider how culture is reproduced; that is, how cultures – even 'broken' or 'toxic' ones – persist and perpetuate. How do people get to learn and *know* 'how we do things around here' when they become part of an organization or group? And how can that become so rigid and stuck?

Culture as lived (vs what's written on the wall in reception), as I'll say many times, is implicit and unspoken in the sense of not being openly described. And for the new employee, culture is a kind of *etiquette*. When new to any situation, most of us are highly motivated to learn the rules, fit in and understand how to operate 'around here'. Remember your first day at a new school? Or being at a social event with rules you didn't know? Knowing that there *are* rules but not knowing what those rules are is very stressful – we may experience a huge urge to run away. So when we're new to an organization and we can't just run away, we're highly motivated to learn the *etiquette*, work out how to fit in and understand how to operate 'around here'.

"When you violate one of our unwritten rules
you'll know it by the unspoken censure."

So newcomers quickly learn to read the lived culture from a range of signs and signals around them – including how people talk, behave, sit, dress, socialize, run meetings, contribute (or not) to them, how they create PowerPoints, what's on the noticeboards, what reception areas look like… and much more. They will take in how things are done, what gets done and what doesn't, the names of things, what *has* a name and what doesn't, how things are measured and valued, what's displayed as important; what's hidden or ignored, and how space, people and things are divided up and organized. All of these are 'languages' of a kind.

As I suggested in the Preface, it doesn't take long for all of this to become natural – after a while people don't notice the quirks and characteristics of where they work. It's become the air they breathe and 'how we do things.'

It's generally only the new joiners who have conscious awareness of the organization's specific culture – but most of these don't have the social status or formal power to comment, let alone be seen to criticize. And it's only with the arrival of a powerful, senior newcomer that this scenario may be challenged. *So it goes on.*

When organizational culture is fully functional, this process of rapid absorption and naturalization by newcomers is a great thing – they quickly pick up the language and, along with it, the unspoken assumptions and thinking that lie beneath. A common language plays a role in group bonding and identity too, signalling belonging, shared experience and common values.

However, cultural norms that remain unchanged because they're hidden can, over time, begin to fossilize. In this state they start to constrain thinking and action and hinder adaptation to changing circumstances. Stable cultures may thus become outdated, limiting or even deeply dysfunctional. Decisions and actions made unconsciously that are shaped by the existing culture often fail to resolve new problems. The stability lent by this invisible cultural propagation means organizations too can fossilize, staying the same even as major changes take place in their operating contexts – economic, social, political, etc. Stories about the demise of Kodak or IBM, for example, may in fact reflect this tendency.

Legacy language holds legacy thinking in place and is itself held in place by habit and unconscious competence – it takes conscious sustained effort to change what essentially 'works'. Under pressure, people may even hang on to it more tightly. In his article, 'Why good companies go bad' (2005), Donald Sull argues that what were once highly functional 'frames' and resources can, over time, become shackles and millstones. And they do this *not by changing* but simply *by virtue of staying the same*. When organizations fail to adapt to new challenges, he says, it's not that they don't see the threat, but that they diligently work to do *more of what worked in the past*.

This is a significant point when sharing an analysis of culture with people inside an organization. It's important to make it clear that any cultural assumptions and norms that now look dysfunctional or wrong were at one time perfect for the organization's circumstances. It's just that the version of the past that those practices and assumptions are rooted in is no longer relevant.

Chapter 2
How can we think about organizational culture?

Different models of culture inevitably lead to different beliefs and tactics for studying, describing and/or measuring organizational culture, and therefore different notions about how it can be shaped or changed. So it's a good idea to have a brief look here at a few examples of models and frameworks for doing so.

Culture as a thing, a concrete business asset

In the Introduction, I outlined what looks like the dominant model of culture: the implied view that it's a *thing* that can be separated from the people within it and re-engineered, like any business asset.

Many commercial culture change services are offered by large consulting companies or specialist agencies, often using a proprietary change method. The initial analysis or discovery phases within these programmes may be explicitly concerned with 'measuring' culture, often via staff surveys or attitude inventory methods. The results may then be benchmarked against a model comprising conceptual cultural dimensions, derived from data gathered over time from other organizations. In line with the need for numbers (and for cross-sector comparisons) such work aims to extrapolate culture – acknowledged as ideas and assumptions as well as practices – from survey answers, either by directly asking 'how is it working here?' or indirectly via sets of attitudes or statements. These methods and their results are quantified, so they meet an important board requirement for evidence-based decision-making. People, boards and investors want numbers and the sense of certainty and legitimacy that they're inclined to offer. This is quite understandable, as significant decisions may be based on this work, and certainly a sizeable culture consultancy marketplace is built around this need.

There are of course many variations in this field, and to find these approaches one only needs to search online for 'corporate culture' and/or 'culture change' and there will be plenty to choose from. Following such analysis, the organization's leadership will typically, again with the help of consultants, lay out how 'our culture' needs to be in the future. Then a programme is devised and implemented to tell people about it, and to encourage or persuade them to change from one set of cultural norms to a new set. While it's perhaps unfair to categorize all of these services into one bucket, what they do seem to share is a belief that cultural change can and should be directed from the top down.

However, despite the best efforts of skilled analysts and consultants, organizational change is famously hard to achieve. There have been estimates of change programme failure rates of between 30% and 70%, and while the facts of these measurements are now disputed, widespread anecdotal reporting of failure is not. It appears that cultures stubbornly resist deliberate attempts to transform them. Perhaps in practice people are not good at articulating their culture in interviews or surveys in a fully revealing way, and/or they're not good at changing their unspoken beliefs, habits and engrained assumptions through being told or encouraged to do so by those in charge, in a top-down manner. Either way, alternatives have clearly been needed and sought.

Culture as an ongoing process of human interaction

As someone once said, 'Not everything that counts can be counted, and not everything that can be counted counts' (attributed to Einstein, but more likely to have first been said by William Bruce Cameron). So despite the advantages of a quantitative approach that I just described, it makes sense also to seek other models and methods to bring unspoken culture to the surface.

There are numerous models of organizational culture that emphasize its *hidden* quality; culture is seen to be implicit and unspoken. But that means it's hard to get insiders to articulate it. To understand a culture, we need to access the informal or lived process – what actually happens and what makes it so.

You wouldn't try to change the way a factory operates without mapping how it currently works, and that means observing not just the formal processes and official protocols, but also what happens in practice. Regardless of the formal and official procedures, most of the time cultural forces just carry on quietly having a powerful, invisible and unconscious influence over collective thinking and action. If the most significant quality of culture is that it's implicit and unspoken, and is therefore for most practical purposes hidden, this for me is its most interesting, difficult and powerful quality.

Let's look at how some others have addressed this challenge. What follows is far from being a comprehensive review of such approaches and is meant just to give a flavour of the range.

First, the influence of scholar and practitioner Edgar Schein (2004) has been and remains significant. He famously outlined a model for thinking about organizational cultures involving three 'levels': 'artifacts', 'espoused beliefs and values' and 'basic underlying assumptions'.

▷ 'Artifacts' comprise the visible, observable elements of an organization's culture, physical environment, how people dress, rituals and celebrations, structures, and processes and so on.

▷ 'Espoused values' are the claims and declarations that the organization makes in public about its values, mission, ethics, strategic priorities and, of course, its culture.

▷ 'Basic and tacit assumptions' underpin all of these, as I've talked about already.

Schein's 2004 book, *Organizational Culture and Leadership* (3rd edition), remains a classic in the field (the first edition was published 1985), covering his view at that time of organizational culture, together with substantial case studies. Flowing from this thinking, Schein was drawn towards a way of making or encouraging cultural change through conversation. In his original approach to culture work, he gives detailed instructions for internal workshops where staff and managers (participants) can gather their observations and ideas about numerous topics based on his three levels model, helping them to collectively create a map of their culture.

The roots of the analytic approach I've developed over the past two decades lie in part within that overall theory of culture offered by Schein.

Next, there's now a flourishing practice in applying ideas of *complex responsive processes* to organizations, with academics and active practitioners together developing theory and consulting practice based in complexity and social science models of human interactions. (See, for example, Mowles 2021.) These regard organizational culture – and indeed organizations themselves – as existing *only* through the everyday interactions of those within them.

In addition, I've recently come across several individual consultants and writers working in this way, developing their own characteristic practice from practice-based methods and theory. These include, for example, Chris Rodgers, the titles of whose books, *Informal Coalitions* (2007) and *The Wiggly World of Organization* (2021), give a clear sense of his distinctive and non-linear approach to the nature of organizations and to engaging with organizational culture. Organizational practitioner Andrew Cocks similarly rejects the dominant model of culture analysis and change that I described at the beginning of this chapter. In his book, *Counting the Dance Steps* (2022), he too advocates purposeful conversations as the only effective way to encourage change. To fuel these conversations, he has devised sets of sensitizing topics and questions to help people themselves become aware of their culture and make sense of their own lived experience.

These are just two of the writers and consultants working in this way; I cannot do justice to their work in this brief description and would recommend you read their (very readable) books for more on these methods. I suspect it's not a coincidence that they, like me, developed their analytic and interventional approaches from the ground up. That is, their practice-based theory and activities have been developed over the course of many years of employment inside large organizations, and/or carrying out practical consulting engagements with them, working directly with individuals, leaders and teams.

Culture as discourse

The linguistic approach I describe in this book has much in common philosophically with that set of models and methods that focus on culture as human interaction. If conversation is the way to evolve an organization's culture, it follows that investigating an existing culture would also comprise interaction and shared discovery involving people at all levels. However, orchestrating unstructured conversations across a large organization is potentially a lengthy and challenging process. Using discourse analysis to point to implicit culture provides a bridge or shortcut between the unconscious reality of lived experience – living *in* it – and the conscious experience of talking *about* it.

The discourse approach to culture that's the subject of this book works by holding a sensitive but systematic and dispassionate mirror up to the organization, allowing hypotheses about the cultural norms visible within its language to be identified. It's then crucial that these hypotheses are *presented to and validated by those involved*. In my experience such analysis is at its most effective when used as a catalyst to widespread 'culture conversations', and where momentum for change then comes from *within* the multitude of people in the organization, or at least from within a critical mass of them. Painting a picture of culture that closely represents how it's lived and felt by those inside it, and in which people can recognize the reality of their day-to-day working lives, is a useful basis for action. In fact, seeing the results of the analysis can alone stimulate a shift in perspective for those on the ground, and they often experience that as exciting and intriguing. As a client put it:

> 'The mere suggestion of how we talk and its implications triggered an immediate desire for action. The truths felt obvious. I think this is a big part of [its] power.'

Such analysis in practice creates rich feedback that prompts sense-making conversations among those intimately involved in all aspects of organizational practice. The systematic and dispassionate nature of the work can give confidence, but the outputs are often felt as personally meaningful and significant. It offers people within a culture insights about that culture that are personally and collectively meaningful – and the effect of those insights on them can be powerful.

In Chapter 3 I'll look at why *language* is a particularly useful form of data for qualitative analysis of organizational culture. First, though, I'll explain what I've called 'the three big culture questions'.

Culture as the answers to three big questions

Let's return to the three big culture questions I proposed in the Introduction and look at them in more detail. To remind you, they are:

- ▶ Who are 'we' and what really matters around here?

- ▶ Who do we assume 'they' are out there (customers, competitors, regulators, students, patients, partner organizations and more), and what do we think of them?

- ▶ How do we 'do' relationships around here – with each other and with 'them' out there?

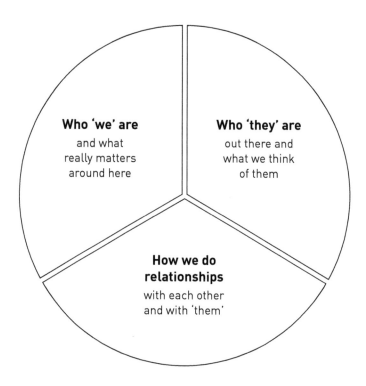

The 'culture pie'

You'll see that the questions in this 'culture pie' refer both to the 'inside' and the 'outside' – 'us' in here and 'them' out there. Organizations don't operate in a vacuum, and it makes sense to me that a framework for thinking about culture should include the notion of how 'others' – those outside some formal or informal boundary – are represented within that culture.

Hence, the simple model of culture that has emerged for me contains not only the organization's internal sense of *identity* – who we are and how we do things – but also the projection or construction of those *outside*, and ideas about how *relationships* with important people and groups outside the organization are to be enacted.

What is 'the organization', though, and where is its boundary? Pragmatically, we'd work at the focal length or level that's needed *and* possible. So if the presenting problem concerns wide-ranging issues, we might attempt to find the commonalities of a whole 'culture' that runs across divisions and silos, or at least across enough of them to allow for useful insight and action. On the other hand, if the issue that needs attention concerns differences or difficulties between two smaller divisions or indeed informal groupings (the 'old hands' and the 'newcomers', for example), then those two subcultures would be the focus of analysis.

No matter how the idea of an organizational culture is carved up, the three culture questions are useful. For a pan-organization analysis, the 'we' might be the legal entity, and the 'they' would be all those externals, such as customers or regulators, who are involved, but not formally inside. For a more granular look at parts of an organization, the 'we' might be, say, legal and compliance, and 'they' are marketing (and, of course, vice versa).

There's one more level of unpacking for these three questions that I want to introduce here:

- ▶ Who are 'we' and what really matters around here?
    - ❏ Who we really believe we are – our truths and identity; the things we believe will always be that way.

- ▶ Who do we assume 'they' are out there (customers, competitors, regulators, students, patients, partner organizations and more), and what do we think of them?
    - ❏ Here I mean the *internal representation* of what and who is 'out there' and how 'we' imagine 'them'. This is *not* the same as what those people or entities *actually* are, but what internal mental models and culture *assume* is the case, as evidenced in language. This perspective doesn't often feature in analysis of culture, yet it's crucial to many operational and strategic decisions for any organization. For example, if you assume your customers are financially savvy, you'll create products for them and address them differently from how you would if you assume they're rather naive or dim.

- ▶ How do we 'do' relationships around here – with each other and with 'them' out there?
    - ❏ You may be wondering why I talk about how we '*do*' relationships, rather than talking about the relationships we

have. The slightly odd construction reflects the way that in discourse analysis, language is always active – it *does* things (see Chapter 3). So the 'doing relationships' idea serves to remind us that we're interested not in what that relationship *is* (as if it's a fixed thing) but in *the way we go about* interacting with and relating to 'them'. Do we, for example, tend to assume a position of superiority? Or do we perhaps offer informality and a degree of intimacy as our default position?

- Again, here I mean the kinds of internal relationships and external stakeholder relationships that are *constructed* in language – the expectations and assumptions that are subtly beamed out. Say our assumption is that 'we' are in charge, and 'you' are to be passive and grateful. Or we assume that, like us, you're only interested in what we can get from each other.

By definition, relationships involve two or more parties, so what actually happens in a particular internal or external interaction depends on how 'they' respond. However, we tend to get the relationships we attract – we implicitly invite specific types of relationships through our language and behaviour. So if we act like a child, we're likely to elicit 'parental' responses from others, for better or worse. If we want a serious romantic relationship but always behave like we just want a quick evening of fun, that's what we'll 'beam out' in our language and actions, and we may never find the lasting love we seek. If we behave forcefully, we may elicit submission – or we may provoke aggression in return.

These three culture questions have proved in practice to be revealing and powerful organizing ideas in unpicking the culture of a group and identifying where it has become dysfunctional, or indeed how and why it's successful. Shared language commonly used within a group gives strong clues about the ideas and beliefs that might answer these questions. In practice, applying a discourse analysis perspective to samples of internal and external language means one can generate *working hypotheses* about shared assumptions and rules of thumb. These are not facts or conclusions about 'its culture', but some reflection of the ideas and shared 'truths' that language choices seem to suggest. A description (without judgement or blame) of what *appear* to be the underlying, taken-for-granted assumptions that people *seem* to be applying in everyday decisions and interactions can then provide powerful and useful feedback to everyone who's part of the culture.

Chapter 3
What's so useful about organizational language?

To analyse culture in a manageable way one needs something to represent it, ideally something that's both rich in meaning and also objectively observable and systematically analysable. Schein's artifacts provide a useful model for this idea. The method I'm describing builds on Schein's model, focusing on an organization's language as a rich 'artifact' that, if analysed systematically, is capable of shedding light on organizational culture quickly, sensitively and efficiently.

Language as a 'super-artifact'

A brief reminder: Schein's artifacts comprise the visible, observable elements of an organization's culture – things such as the physical space, how people dress, rituals and celebrations, structures and processes. These are distinguished from what he calls 'espoused values' – the claims and declarations that the organization makes in public about its values, mission, ethics, strategic priorities and, of course, its culture. In our work, we use the labels 'everyday language' or 'surface language' for language artifacts, and refer to espoused values as 'claims and wishes'. We use both forms of language as data to help point to Schein's third category, 'basic underlying assumptions'.

As an artifact, much organizational language sits on the surface, looking like it has no depth or significance – it's just commonplace 'business as usual'. People look *through* such language, seeking only its content, not *at* it. But, in fact, this language holds telling clues about the shape and the nature of the culture beneath – to quote a colleague and client, 'Language is the data of culture'.

In this context, *all* the organization's language is potentially relevant: written and spoken, formal and informal, internally and externally directed, everyday and 'special'. It includes 'claims and wishes' items such as public statements of values and culture – not as facts about the organization or culture, but as a specific kind of cultural artifact.

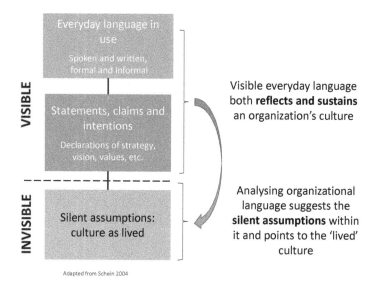

Adapted from Schein 2004

An organization's implicit view of the world is embedded in how its people automatically talk with and write to each other every day, about things such as customers, products and markets, processes, people – in fact everything. As we've seen, such a world view is difficult for those inside an organization to hold in awareness, because it's taken for granted.

I've come to think of language as a 'super-artifact' as it's such a useful proxy for culture. As an organizational cultural artifact, language is:

> **Important.** Many organizations don't have co-located staff or physical premises, or even shared time zones, but language is always used in some way to coordinate action – it's the very essence of 'organization'.

▷ **Well distributed.** Everyone uses language, throughout the organization, in all areas and departments, written and spoken, formal and informal texts.

▷ **Freely available as data, and non-disruptive to collect.** Language can for the most part be gathered for analysis off-site. Some live observations and conversations are helpful, but most of our data-gathering processes don't intrude on normal organizational activities.

▷ **Largely resistant to researcher effect.** While it can be useful to generate some language data using interviews or observation, most of our analysis is carried out on materials that already exist in the organization. This means data has been produced as part of business as usual and not for the purposes of research – sometimes termed 'naturally occurring' data.

▷ **A potent carrier of culture.** Language, as a carrier of culture, gets everywhere and colours everything. So, like taking phials of water from a swimming pool to test the chemical balance of the whole pool, you don't need to analyse it all. If attempting to get the sense of a shared culture across a large part of an organization, you can therefore include material from a large number of teams/divisions/locations in an analysis, using the principles of good qualitative sampling.

Lastly, and perhaps most relevant of all:

▷ **Language can be analysed using a set of systematic, empirically based methods.** This can produce vivid and compelling evidence and highly meaningful findings – findings that are easily understood and used by people throughout the organization. I'm referring here to the happy marriage of the characteristics of language as a cultural artifact with the approach to language developed in academic social sciences over the past few decades and broadly known as 'discourse analysis'.

Discourse analysis and how can it reveal culture

As I outlined in the Introduction, discourse analysis comprises a wide range of academic thinking and research methods. Its core ideas have arisen over the past four decades, emerging almost simultaneously in academia across various social sciences, linguistics, history, political studies, philosophy and literary criticism. As a method, it draws on empirical scientific work in sociolinguistics, social psychology, sociology and other fields.

The definition of the word 'discourse' itself is contested, but this simple definition gives the sense in which I use it here:

> '[Discourse is] *a particular way of talking about and understanding the world (or an aspect of the world).'* Jørgensen and Phillips 2002 p. 1

There are many different academic methods and models within this field, and inevitable disagreements and tensions across the academic disciplines engaged in it. However, the diversity of models under the broad heading of 'discourse analysis' means that many analytic tools are available. In my own applied practice over the past two decades, I've adopted and adapted numerous discourse analytic methods, drawing particularly from Discursive Psychology, Critical Discourse Analysis and Conversation Analysis.

Most discursive approaches share a few common threads, and for our purposes the following are the most useful to know about.

Language is active and constructive

'Discourse analysis' at root says that language doesn't (just) *describe* things, but it *does* things. It 'constructs' our realities, especially in making certain things seem inevitable, or natural. That is, language isn't a transparent and neutral medium through which we communicate information or describe things that just 'are'. It's *active* – we use language choices to *do* things socially, culturally and politically, to construct and maintain a certain view of the world (even if we do all this unconsciously).

The shifts in language seen in some English-speaking cultures away from 'marking' job roles as held by a man or a woman are a good example of how making a cultural distinction becomes outdated and the language shifts along with it. So we now hear about 'actors' (who may identify as male *or* female) at least as often as we see 'actor' and 'actress' used as opposing terms. We also less often hear the terms 'male nurse' or 'lady doctor' than in the past, as our collective sense has grown that gendering jobs is wrong.

Similarly, we may not be aware of it, but language normalizes certain relationships and ways of being. For example, language:

▶ Can set up opposites, creating an *apparent* either/or choice ('talk' vs 'action'; 'academic' vs 'real world'; 'working' vs 'retired').

▶ Can make things seem 'factual' – true, objective, real. (Scientific discourse does this in several ways, but typically by removing the scientists themselves from the discourse – so we read 'the fluid was heated to 30 degrees' and not 'I heated the fluid to 30 degrees'.)

▶ Can position a person or group in a particular way. (Am I a mother of two? A researcher? A business owner? An author? A British citizen? A dog owner? I'm all of those, but each label positions me in a certain way. If I'm described as a 'mother of two' or a 'dog owner' in a context where my identity as an 'author' is, to me, more relevant, I'll hear the implications and may resist this categorization.)

▶ Discourse might enshrine positions of inclusion and exclusion. (I'll look in Chapter 5 at the use of pronouns such as 'we/they/you' and 'us/them', and the work these do within an organizational culture.)

▶ Discourse can also represent and reproduce relationships of power. (Someone who persists in calling you by a name you don't choose for yourself is exerting a certain power. In some circumstances we recognize this power and may categorize it as, say, bullying. See also Chapter 6.)

Work can also be done by what's *not* said overtly; for example, just one half of a binary might be spoken, leaving the other unspoken but implied, and still performing work. As an example, the phrase 'right people, right skills, right place and right time' used repeatedly as a *future* aim within a particular client organization implicitly constructed *current* staff as 'wrong people, with the wrong skills, in the wrong place, at the wrong time'.

Detail and structure matter, not just words

Discourse analysis allows us to read social and cultural meaning from the way in which language is *used* in real life, rather than how words are defined in the dictionary. We need to be alert to the role of words/lexicon, of course, but also to the smallest elements of structure, the most subtle resources we have as users of language – things such as pauses, how we order items in a list, whether we use a passive or active (as in the science discourse example above), and much more. Absences too, are relevant

– terms, phrases or topics that might be expected in a certain context, but that are absent.

The focus in discourse analysis is often on micro things – the structure and detail of language – but these are interesting because of what they reveal about much bigger, deeper things. In the organizational context we look for clues about assumptions and taken-for-granted ideas that might underpin specific patterns of language, and what certain words used in particular contexts might indicate about underlying norms and the characteristic patterning of everyday interaction.

Every language choice carries meaning

Discourse analysis is especially powerful when used comparatively. So asking 'how it could be otherwise' for a particular text, or even word, helps give distance and lets us see what's being done with the language we're looking at. This question is an immensely powerful thinking tool for this work (see Example 3).

Every detail of language usage is meaningful because, where a choice is made, there was always the possibility for different choice, and it's therefore meaningful. Note again that I'm not talking about conscious or deliberate 'choice' here, but the automatic and unthinking choices we all make when we decide to say, for example, actor and not actress when referring to a female performer.

So in analysing language, we're always asking what language *choices* are being made, and what the alternatives might have been. (Note: we're asking about alternatives to the language currently being used as a way to see its implications more clearly, not to offer suggestions for change.)

Power, ideology and normalization

As I mentioned in the Introduction, discourse analytic methods are often used to study existing relationships of power and how the distribution of resources can be made to seem 'natural' through discourse. Ideas embedded in habitual, everyday language can easily develop an 'unremarkable' quality and this is one way in which analysing discourse is so valuable in excavating the unquestioned rules and unspoken norms of an organization. There's a rich academic literature covering this area, especially in the work of Norman Fairclough (see, for example, 2003), who calls this process 'naturalization'.

Everyday language is very absorbent of culture – so analysing language carefully will point to what's being taken for granted and *not* said. It suggests the frames of reference, ideas and beliefs – about ourselves, others and our relationship – that are unspoken but that must be there in order for that language to make sense.

If you'd like to know more about discourse analysis, there are several books and papers in the References section at the end of this book.

————

In Section I, I've set out the groundwork for what follows – why organizational culture matters, some different ways to think about it and why I believe that language offers a rich and powerful way to access culture in a way that makes it accessible to everyone involved in it. Now we can move on to the process itself, and what language can tell us about culture.

SECTION II:

WHAT ORGANIZATIONAL TALK CAN TELL US

In the first chapter in this section, I'll outline an overall approach to gathering organizational language and analysing it using discourse analysis principles.

The remaining three chapters describe a selection of specific linguistic clues to culture – some features you can look for that give clues to our three big cultural questions, arranged in chapters by question.

Chapter 4
Turning everyday language into data

Cultural clues are all around us in an organization's language. I think of it as 'the depth on the surface'; innocuous, transparent-looking everyday language that usually gets ignored, but that can be examined for its deep and significant meaning.

Practically, then, how can one go about mining it for insight? What follows is the broad outline of a typical research approach that we use in consulting.

Defining and collecting data

Gathering samples of language to use as data

- ▶ Internal language of all kinds is relevant: written and spoken, formal and informal, internally and externally directed, everyday and 'special', 'naturally occurring' and generated for the enquiry.

- ▶ Externally directed language might be relevant too, depending on the brief and the issue that's being investigated.

- ▶ 'Naturally occurring' for these purposes means language that has been produced with no reference at all to the research or researcher. This will often have been produced before the research and is preserved in documents or other written forms, such as reports and presentations, minutes, intranet pages or in recordings of past exchanges such as customer calls.

▶ This is treated differently in analysis from language that's produced *for* the research (interviews or conversations), or is *likely* to be affected or shaped by it, even if marginally (such as observation of meetings, and listening in to live calls in a call centre while sitting alongside the agent taking them).

▶ A note on visual images as data: my focus is on verbal language for the reasons I laid out earlier – accessibility, ubiquity and so on – but it's impossible to ignore the role played by images as language data too. Examples of these, such as those found in advertising, or in internal communications, posters on walls and so on, would be included in the analysis where relevant.

Just as an archaeologist views faint marks in the mud, the contents of ancient rubbish tips and scattered bits of detritus as valuable data (as well as the beautiful found objects), we treat an organization's language 'litter' – the mass of language materials produced every day – as highly valuable and telling data (as well as the crafted pieces that are statements of intent and of espoused values). The unnoticed, unremarked and 'unimportant' can often be the most telling.

Internal language data might include, for example:

▶ Formal strategy and key policy documents and presentations, and high-level statements of values, purpose, intent, etc.
  ❑ Note that the latter are important texts for analysis but are not the best language data for understanding a culture. They're examples of the culture in action, not a definitive description of it.

▶ Induction materials.
  ❑ Again, this material is likely to reflect formal elements of the espoused culture, such as vision and values. The new employee will, of course, also experience the hidden and messy world of the organization as they begin to interact with others and become immersed in the lived culture.

- Samples of internal memos, minutes, reports and emails.

- Existing customer/stakeholder research and consultation documents.

- Organizational charts, job titles and descriptions.

- Intranet pages, internal newsletters, internal announcements.

- Notices pasted on to walls or noticeboards.

- Conversations between colleagues, language used in meetings, presentations, etc.

Data showing organizational culture interacting with the outside world (if relevant) might include:

- The public website

- Social media

- Advertising and customer/user communications (if relevant)

- External newsletters

- Recruitment ads

Generating language data through unstructured conversations

- Informal conversations can produce very useful language data, especially if fully unstructured. Ideally, we want to generate talk that's driven by speakers themselves, including what they choose to talk about and how, and not by an interviewer's questions.

- So we would *not* ask questions such as, 'What's the culture like here?' Rather, we'd invite people simply to talk about their own role, the company and current issues, imposing as little structure and language of our own on to it as possible. So 'tell me about your work' might be a typical starting prompt.

- These conversations also begin the process of generating a broader 'culture conversation' within the organization, so have a dual role. The same applies to the observation of meetings, call centre interactions and so on.

Analysing this data by looking for *patterns*

In this chapter I'll set out the first stage of analysis, a trawl for major features and possible clues to cultural norms. This is followed by finer grained or 'forensic' language analysis against our three culture questions: *Who we are, who they are, how we do relationships*. The finer grained analysis is covered in later chapters.

This is the place to mention briefly the implications of developments in artificial intelligence (AI) and tools such as ChatGPT. At Linguistic Landscapes, our approach is generally to work with skilled human qualitative discourse analysts. These are people trained and experienced in being open to patterns across a wide range of linguistic features, not just words, and who are also trained in developing ideas about the significance of those patterns for the client's issue.

In our consulting work, though, we've also developed several ways of harnessing the power of computing to do what it's good at – such as seeing patterns in vast arrays of language data that are otherwise hard to see – while keeping a firm human hand on both the design of the research and ultimately on its interpretation.

We use other computer-assisted methods that have been developing in linguistics for the past few decades, including those drawn from corpus linguistics and Natural Language Processing (a sub-field of AI). The relevance and power of AI will undoubtedly grow, and I imagine that we'll continue to develop ways to employ it. However, culture is a profoundly human phenomenon, and I suspect AI-assisted discourse analysis work for organizations will still, in the foreseeable future, depend for its value on the human relationships and conversations that are attached to and flow from it.

A note on patterns and examples: please note that I've often used single examples of language to illustrate a point or set of findings. However, these are all examples drawn from the wider patterns from which we drew conclusions – they did not stand alone.

Getting started: a trawl for major features and clues

Doing discourse analysis means making the familiar strange – developing an anthropologist's curiosity and eye. So we'd take a first scan of what we have. What sticks out? What strikes us? This work must be systematic, but one must also use gut feeling and one's human experience as a speaker of the language.

These are some broad initial questions to ask about the material:

- Who or what are major 'actors' in the organizational discourse? This doesn't mean who actually 'acts' in the organization, but those things that appear significant and active in this language. Actors in this sense may also not be people at all but be entities, functions or even places:
  - Who and what appears? And how exactly are they referred to?
  - 'Actors' can be individuals, groups of people, organizations, and more: 'Excom', 'Mr Saunders', 'Ken', 'our colleagues at the other end of the building', 'Miss Lucy'.
  - They may be people or groups currently involved in the organization, or key figures or ideas from within the organization's past, given current relevance by their continued presence in discourse.
  - Customers/users/patients/citizens, 'the customer', or perhaps insider shorthand for such: 'UPBs', 'a post-Epsilon case', 'a Gold'.
  - The regulator/the City/the markets.
  - Investors/funders/shareholders.
  - Places/buildings/functions as actors: Head Office, 'The Tower', 'the business', 'Glasgow', 'Compliance', 'the 40th floor'.
  - They can even be documents or policies, with a meaning internally that may baffle the outsider – a 'Section 141 notice'.
  - Systems and technologies too can appear in discourse as actors: for example, Horizon was the computer system that proved to be disastrously faulty in the UK Post Office scandal. It became a significant discursive actor within the Post Office itself but also in the UK government, judiciary, press and so on as the scandal unfolded.

- Are there recurring terms, stories, jokes or expressions? For example:
  - Recurring tales/jokes (e.g. about senior leaders/certain groups/certain events).
  - Recurring mantras or repeated quotes, perhaps from a founder figure or a famous outsider.
  - Linguistic 'hotspots' – clearly contested terms or ideas ('professional/unprofessional' and other binaries such as 'clinical' vs 'non-clinical' staff).

- ▶ Can you identify any distinctive/characteristic/unusual language styles or features? For example:
  - ❑ Swearing, hyper-politeness, use of slang, joking language as standard.
  - ❑ Formal/informal language as the organizational norm.
  - ❑ Ellipsis (leaving things out and treating them as assumed), intimacy, conversationality.
  - ❑ Flowery or elaborate language (ask – what work is this doing?).
  - ❑ Group-specific language that excludes others – including, for example, acronyms, local slang, impenetrable and/or technical language used *outside* technical environments.
  - ❑ Euphemisms.
  - ❑ Company-specific acronyms or shorthand/slang.
  - ❑ Moral discourse – judgemental language, extremes such as 'disgusting, shocking.'
  - ❑ 'Bossy' or 'needy' sounding language (both are parent-child language forms).

It's best not to over-interpret at this stage. We see this as simply noticing, observing, reflecting and noting for now.

Example 1: The first trawl through a UK government organization's internal language

Initial observations:

Who or what are major actors in the organizational drama?

- ▶ The IT system is *the* system by which the work of the organization gets done – it dominates talk about the work of the organization, dwarfing other agents and actors, human or otherwise.

- ▶ Stats, data and numerical targets are visible *everywhere* – on walls, in the lobby, in conversations.

- ▶ Peculiar use of the term 'customers' – seems to refer to some customers only, not all.

- ▶ Others who are technically also 'customers' are unnamed, or defined only in terms of the organization's schemes, or the IT and processing system.

Recurring terms, stories, jokes or expressions?

▶ Endless stories of a lost and golden age – wistfulness and regret. Some quiet rebellion: 'It doesn't have to be the way it is now'.

▶ Deep disappointment around 'whole case working', as an unfulfilled promise made by a past leader.

▶ A particular emotion around 'locked' standard letters – a new system that allowed no tailoring of tone or content for an individual customer by the staff member.

▶ Some people have the unusual job title 'Gatekeeper'.

Any distinctive/characteristic/unusual language styles or features?

▶ Submissive language: 'We have no choice'. 'It has to be this way or we'll be punished severely'. 'It's the regulations'.

▶ System-derived language is pervasive inside the organization – and leaks copiously to the outside.

▶ Consistent *opposition* of 'the system' to all kinds of human qualities – *thinking, intelligence, compassion*.

▶ Huge concern with detail and fine granularity – everyone, even senior managers, focused at a micro level.

Example 2: A first set of language observations from work with a UK local authority

The organization was aware it had a 'culture problem' but needed help to define and address it and these were our initial linguistic observations. This looks like a random collection of features, but the seeds of what we later developed as findings are, as so often, in this first trawl:

▶ Frequent use of imperatives, and rules, rules, rules everywhere.

▶ Relationships constructed as parent-child across the organization.

- ▶ Some interesting naming and references to HQ – ivory tower, the palace in the sky.

- ▶ A dominant spatial metaphor: constant reference to up, down, above, below, horizontal.

- ▶ Pronouns: 'we' usually refers to a small close group; very little use of whole-organization 'we'.

- ▶ Narratives and characters: and episodic form, like a soap opera – things happen, people come and go, but little fundamental changes.

- ▶ Organization of texts: striking accumulation in the intranet of similar-sounding but different directives, policies, training materials, etc., old and new.

As analysts, we ask ourselves:

- ▶ *What strikes you about these observations?* Look closely when an example of language catches your eye – notice how it makes you feel, or the 'voice' it has, then see if you can identify *why* you get that feeling. For example:
  - ❏ Do emails between colleagues always sound like messages between teenagers? Or are they extra-super polite? Or are they brief, to the point of feeling abrupt? Can you spot what it is about them that make them sound like this? Is this part of a wider pattern? Where else do you see or feel this kind of language? And where within the organization is it different?
  - ❏ What's being *done* when people use the term 'the competition'? And what about 'the customer'? Is it fear? Annoyance? Contempt? (We've seen all of these.) *How* does the language give you that sense?

- ▶ *How do these observations compare with other organizations you know or have worked in?* Ask what alternative language people *could* be using ('how could it be otherwise'). In order to see clearly the choices that people within a particular cultural context are implicitly making in the way that they talk about a key idea – say, the term 'borrowing' used within financial services company

– one needs to look at how else borrowing could feasibly be talked about, in another company, or perhaps by a customer.

Example 3: Using the 'how could it be otherwise?' test

We noticed a recurrent word – 'drive/driving' – being used within a division of a US corporate bank and being applied to numerous activities. So we'd see 'driving growth', 'driving acquisition' and, most interestingly, 'driving reappraisal'.

▶ The context was that the company's marketers wanted ex-customers to think again about the brand – to 'reappraise' it.

▶ The term used for activity aimed at this end was *driving reappraisal*.

▶ This seemed to position the customer as *passive* and as the *target* of the company's rather macho activities – as if they lacked any self-determination or agency.

How could it be otherwise? How might the same content be expressed differently? In this exercise one is looking for a perfectly reasonable alternative form of language that another similar organization might use. This comparison allows us to see (and to show others) the choices that are being made.

▶ For example, we could rewrite it as '*inviting* reappraisal' or '*encouraging* reappraisal' – both would be perfectly reasonable alternative phrases (and might even be in use in other organizations).

▶ These phrases construct a different kind of relationship, in which the customer retains agency.

▶ So, saying 'driving reappraisal' isn't *inevitable*, or just what *anyone in any business would say* – it's potentially a tiny clue to the cultural patterning of people's interactions, and how they collectively tend to view themselves and their customers, in a certain way.

> If a sense of macho forcefulness is, in cultural terms, a central organizing theme for that culture, we'd expect to see it reflected in other language forms too, as a pattern. That is, frequent use of rather muscular, forceful language, even in contexts that don't seem to justify it.

Making first observations and ideas explicit is helpful, as the analyst quickly starts to get a sense for something that's particular to this culture, and even where some cultural issues might be. *However* – one needs to resist moving too quickly to judgement! There's a lot more to do and look at in the language.

Going deeper: language forensics

So far, we've got a sense for the main features of this language landscape. Now we need to go in closer to develop a deeper sense of the cultural imperatives, and core cultural assumptions that define the culture that's being examined.

I often think about this approach to culture analysis as 'language forensics'; closely inspecting a set of messy and unstructured material, looking for tiny clues that, as a pattern, might reflect the wider patterning of interaction that we can think of as organizational culture. We're seeking a picture of what might be there – and/or might *once* have been there – for the surface details to make sense.

In the next three chapters I've clustered together some of the language features that we've found especially revealing, under the headings of the three culture questions I outlined earlier. This is not a comprehensive list of hard and fast linguistic objects but a selection of technical language features and patterns that we've often found to be relevant when analysing organizational culture through discourse.

For you the reader, why might spotting linguistic features that happen to have technical names matter, or indeed help? You might look at what emerges from a first trawl of your own organizational language, and consider the three cultural questions and feel that's enough to begin some conversations with colleagues and leaders. If you want to, though, going further into the linguistics provides a way of *focusing* and *codifying*, and, through this, a way to identify and begin to discuss issues of culture.

The worlds of linguistics and discourse analysis are full of wonderful notions that, once explained, are often familiar to us – we just don't always know the terminology, or that something is indeed a 'thing'. So, terms such as hedging, modality and intensifiers point to useful ideas for our purposes, and you'll recognize the patterns these refer to, shown in the examples later. You'll also find some familiar ideas that many will have first encountered at school, such as pronouns, passive/active forms and metaphor.

The linguistic ideas and features explained in the next three chapters are best seen as sensitizing categories. If you're interested in experimenting with this, it's less important to *label* something you notice in your organization's language using one of these categories than it is to sensitize your eyes and ears to such ideas. That way you might identify relevant idiosyncrasies within your culture, and focus on what they can tell you, especially in the light of the concerns about culture that led you to do this work in the first place.

Codifying and labelling patterns does, however, make it easier to explain to others what you think you see, to agree a common language, and to work together on implications and actions. So the technical terms may be useful when nothing else is exact enough to capture what you notice.

For each of the categories of language featured in these chapters, I'll explain why that kind of language matters, how it might help in reading a particular organizational culture, and what to look out for, along with some examples.

Note – not all these categories or features will be relevant or useful for a particular culture, and there's often a degree of overlap. This is designed as a prompt list to stimulate your thinking and to illustrate some unspoken qualities of culture that language can point to when examined at this level.

Two reminders:

> ▶ The three questions – who are we/who are they/how do we do relationships? – refer to the *internal representation* of what and who is 'out there', and the way relationships are constructed or implied. This is not what they *actually* are, but what the organizational culture seems to assume is the case, as evidenced in language.

We're looking for what's being treated as normal, and the overall world view or narrative that's being sustained internally.

▶ No matter which linguistic scent trail you're following, remember to ask what *choices* are being made. Asking 'how could it be otherwise?' will help you see them.

Chapter 5
Culture question 1: Who are 'we' and what matters around here?

This is the longest of the three detailed sections, as we focus here on the shared sense of self. How can we hypothesize from the organization's idiosyncratic language the 'sense of self' that an organization or group holds, and which it reproduces, even as its environment changes and newcomers arrive? And what about internal subcultures or groupings – how do they feature?

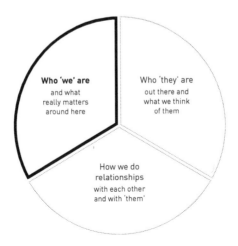

Who 'we' are
and what
really matters
around here

Who 'they' are
out there and
what we think
of them

How we do
relationships
with each other
and with 'them'

Here are the language features and patterns covered in this chapter that give clues to some aspects of identity:

- ▶ Pronouns and labels
- ▶ Dominant and competing discourses
- ▶ 'Professional' and 'unprofessional'
- ▶ Stories
- ▶ Metaphor

Pronouns and labels

A significant thing to notice in looking at 'who we think we are' is to ask exactly who counts as 'we'. It's also good to consider how many different 'we' groups there are, and how they relate to each other.

Note that in discourse analysis the smallest features can be important and telling. Pronouns seem insignificant, so no one pays real attention to them or monitors their own use of them, but they 'leak' unspoken beliefs, norms and assumptions. They're often one of the first things we look at when beginning an analysis.

❖ Why this matters

Groups, tribes and boundaries – important organizational issues are often hidden in plain sight, in small clues such as the use of 'we', often ignored (too familiar to notice) and yet entirely visible – marking the boundaries that *matter*, internal and external, and whether formal and informal. Divisions and labels are, of course, tied in closely with questions of power, and with mutual respect (or lack of it) across boundaries.

Coherence and fragmentation – looking closely at pronouns gives us a sense of who in practice people regard as their own 'we' group. This can range from the whole international organization to a tiny immediate group of colleagues. Note that we're not making a judgement here about what's right or good for a particular organization – you'll be able to think through the implications of what emerges.

Engagement – along with other details, analysis of 'we' and 'they' groups gives *some* information about how engaged people are with the organizational endeavour, where their loyalties lie, etc. Or at least it hints at the degree of 'engagement' that it's appropriate or necessary to display within the culture.

❖ What to look out for

Pronouns

What boundaries can you see expressed in small details of language, especially pronouns? Pronouns – tiny and usually unconsciously used words – are very revealing of how people think and operate within organizations. Who counts as 'we' and who's regarded as 'they'? Where are the lines drawn? People, grades/levels, departments (e.g. legal), head office, customers, regulators, end users, etc. Inside and outside? We've seen both extremes: where the 'we' group is a small team, or where 'we' refers to the whole organization.

Pronouns are not the only powerful way to see engagement or fragmentation, but it's always worth looking at 'we' groups and the language surrounding them.

For example:

> In Organizations S and H we noticed an unusually low level of what we'd call the 'whole-organization we'. In fact, the relevant 'we' for most people in the study was confined to the tiny subgroup of their immediate team. In both cases there was significant emotion attached to the small 'we' – although it wasn't always positive emotion. Being 'siloed' is common, of course, but what was noticeable here was the extreme to which this pronoun use applied in this organization.

> At the opposite extreme, at Organization A it was noticeable how people at all levels constantly used 'us' to mean the *whole* global company. You might read this as high staff engagement, or perhaps as indicative of a cultural norm demanding unquestioning loyalty. The observation alone won't tell you, but as one of a range of language clues you'd log this use of 'we' as something to be held in mind and later linked with any other relevant observations, should these arise.

> We/they/us tensions can be evident very quickly if you see pronouns slipping around – when one voice or group assumes a 'we' that excludes another, for example.

▶ Note that *we/you* or *we/them* boundaries are not always drawn where you'd expect them to be – look for official and unofficial groupings and invisible barriers. Residues of corporate history may also be preserved in groups/boundary markers – and if it's there it's good to think about the significance of this. For example, 'we' may be 'old hands', while 'they' are 'invaders'. See also the section on labels below.

▶ More recently, pronoun use as a personal choice has become a matter for public debate, and the addition of a pronoun identity (*she/her* or *they/their*, for example) to the end of email signatures and profiles has introduced another form of linguistic data into this kind of work. What does it mean within an organizational culture to add this to your emails? And what does it mean within that culture to *not* do so?

▶ There's one more context in which pronouns can be especially problematic – where groups such as HR and other corporate functions need to make declarations to the organization on behalf of the leadership. It's too easy to be ambiguous and inconsistent or to grandly sweep the entire staff into an assumed whole-group 'we', which they may reject or not recognize, or they may hear as a patronizing nursery school 'we'. People may not be able to articulate what they don't like about *'we always consider our colleagues'* and similar statements, but they feel and react to the effects anyway.

Labels

How are formal and informal groups and divisions separated out in language and labelled? Look for official and unofficial groups, and for official and unofficial labels.

▶ How do groups commonly refer to each other? ('Head Office', 'the 40th floor', 'our colleagues at the other end of the building', 'Susan's private office', 'The Tower', 'the business', 'Stephen's world', 'the line', 'Field').

▶ What judgements or evaluations, if any, seem to be embedded in these labels? For example, *we* the 'professionals' vs *them* with the 'non-jobs' (this is a real example from within a professional setting and was part of a discourse of open intolerance of difference). In

TV production, the label 'the talent' refers to those who appear in front of the camera – actors, presenters and so on. This is so familiar to those in the industry that they probably don't hear the implication that hangs in the discourse; that is, that everyone else involved in making programmes *lacks* talent.

▷ What can the organization chart, job titles and divisional names tell you? These can be very revealing too.

Dominant and competing discourses

One of the ways in which the unofficial power and influence structures within the organization can be read is from the language used every day. Sometimes you can see that the internal language of the whole organization (or significant parts of it) is influenced by a certain 'discourse', especially the expert discourse of a professional group such as IT, sales, marketing or compliance.

In essence, discourses are distinctive versions of 'common sense' or characteristic ways of making sense of the world. They offer frameworks for inference and judgement about what things mean, what's right and what's wrong, what's acceptable and not acceptable, and what flows logically from what.

❖ Why this matters

The dominance of an organization's language by one or two discourses is not just a question of whose jargon gets to be used (and therefore whose jargon the rest of the organization has to learn) – it goes much deeper than that. While we're picking up certain terms, and the correct ways of using them, we also absorb the ways of thinking and values that are embedded in them. And, crucially, discourses – certain ways of speaking and thinking – both allow and constrain certain ideas. We're both facilitated and restricted by the language and ideas existing within a particular discourse.

For example, a colleague tells me that the head of a significant global business that had begun as a single retail store had at one time forbidden the use of certain terms, including 'turnover', which she insisted should be called 'takings'. It was arguably both an attempt to construct herself as 'just a shopkeeper' and an attempt to demean financial language that she saw as unacceptably masculine.

Controlling the discourse is a form of power that's harder to challenge than some other forms, since language can be dismissed as unimportant or 'just words' – but this is demonstrably not the case.

❖ What to look out for

Broadly, we're looking for patterns of language that seem to be associated with key terms and also with shared patterns of meaning and taken-for-granted ideas of the world. For example:

> ▸ Western medical discourse features key terms and constructs, such as *patients, symptoms, diagnosis,* and a set of taken-for-granted ideas about the body, health, how issues like pain should be dealt with, how new ideas are to be evaluated and so on.

> ▸ Compare this, say, with the discourse of traditional folk medicine (or the ancient discourse of witchcraft), which would have an entirely different set of terms for the same ideas (folk medicine uses terms such as *sufferers, manifestations* and *assessment,* for example). It would also work with different underlying models and explanations for the same phenomenon, such as pain – in traditional medicine, pain may be seen as a manifestation of imbalances in the body, mind and spirit.

Discourses don't use just different terms for the same things but are entirely different ways of making meaning (i.e. thinking and understanding). What I'm referring to here as 'discourses' are sometimes known as 'linguistic repertoires' or 'interpretative repertoires' – terms originating in discursive psychology (Potter and Wetherell 1987). A repertoire might include a distinctive lexicon, a set of grammatical or stylistic features, certain images, metaphors, idioms, stories and categories.

Repertoires are a mix of content (such as 'typical' topics or lines of argument) and form (characteristic use of grammatical features such as tense and voice and specific choice of lexicon; use of numbers, graphs, etc.). Importantly, they define a set of mental boxes or categories into which things or people can be put. They also entail different values, criteria for judgement and ways of making sense of the same things. For example:

> ▸ Consider the discourse of marketing, with its characteristic lexicon of *consumers, targeting, campaign, positioning, loyalists,*

share of wallet, etc. and an underlying logic about what matters and how to do things. In the marketing discourse it's entirely proper and appropriate to aim, for example, to use psychological understanding to persuade people to buy certain goods and services that they might not otherwise have bought. Such activity would be constructed as *professional* and to be *respected*. In other discourses, however, this activity might be judged and constructed as *misguided*, *exploitative*, or simply '*wrong*'.

We're all familiar with distinctive discourses we come across in everyday life, like those of politics, medicine, law, the police, news reporting and more. Turn on news radio, listen for a couple of minutes and chances are you'll be able to work out the occupation of the speakers, or the topic under discussion, just from a few terms and turns of phrase. In the UK police discourse, for example, officers never search a *house* or a *flat*, they search '*an address*', and so on.

The full range of repertoires or discourses available to each of us offers a palette of sense-making devices: ways of talking and ways of thinking that can be put together in specific situations to make our case, explain our own actions, predict what might happen next and so on. How we use them is often not a conscious decision but is shaped by the discourses that we're exposed to in our everyday lives. And the same applies to the range of discourses or repertoires you might experience within an organization.

Let's now look at a few distinctive discourses that commonly turn up in organizations.

Bureaucratic discourse

'Bureaucracy' is the formal codification of rational organization and is characterized by legal rules, a salaried administrative staff, the specialization of function, authority of the office and not the person, the keeping of written records and documents, and is where the formal dimensions of rule and administration are paramount (see, for example, Weber 1922).

One of bureaucracy's key features is that it's the *job role*, and not the person filling it, that matters; that person is regarded as replaceable. So a concern with processes and roles as dominant actors in the discourse (rather than people or individuals) is typical. For example:

- British civil servants are inclined at times to refer to colleagues by grade (i.e. 'the Grade 6 in X department') rather than anything more individual.

- At a major oil company I worked with, people's job titles had no words at all – each was just a string of letters and numbers. Once inside, one learned to read the code and to realize that the shorter the string, the more powerful and important was the role, and therefore the person currently in it.

These days, we tend to regard a bureaucratic discourse as formal, old-school and 'corporate'. Typically it would be characterized by:

- Nominalizations (processes turned into nouns – such as *engagement*) and indirect language forms, both of which effectively anonymize actions and decisions ('it was decided that').

- Long Latin-derived English words and formal structures are more likely to be used than simpler, more accessible discourse: 'subject to the admittance of the claim, the amount payable will be...' (rather than 'if we agree with your claim we will pay you £xxx').

Both these language features appear again in the section on formality in Chapter 7.

Managerial discourse

This has been the dominant discourse in most commercial organizations since the first half of the 20th century. It regards management techniques and practices as essential to one of its central concerns: the efficient and effective functioning of organizations. The discourse of managerialism is characterized by constructs such as *efficiency, performance, accountability* and *control*, and by the use of *metrics* to measure all of these.

Managerialism is increasingly seen in the government and public sector in the UK. We're so familiar with it in business that we don't normally pay any attention to it, so it's more noticeable when it enters an existing and different discourse in this way. For example:

- Within the UK's National Health Service, over the past 20 or 30 years there has been a steady rise in the discourse of management, with its distinctive lexicon of *'delivery', 'programme', 'service users', 'efficiency'*, etc. This sits alongside the traditional discourse of medicine – *'treat', 'care for', 'help', 'patients'* and so on. The juxtaposition of these two discourses is rather uneasy, not least because, as I've said, discourses are closely connected with how things are evaluated; that is, what matters and why, how much it costs, and how 'cost' should even be measured - and this is inevitably political.

Marketing discourse/the discourse of marketization

As we saw in the example earlier in this section, the discourse of marketing has a characteristic lexicon of *customers, consumers, targeting, campaign, positioning, loyalists* and so on, and characteristic ways of deciding what matters and what does not. This discourse will be very familiar to many working in commercial organizations, even those not carrying out marketing roles. As we saw for managerialism, in the UK this discourse is increasingly present in domains previously seen as outside the market, such as education. Some schools are now limited companies, and universities are increasingly constructing students as 'customers' who need to be attracted, satisfied and retained. And this is similarly an uneasy mix.

Technical/expert discourses (e.g. finance, law)

In many organizations there will be a single dominant form of expertise, whether that's technology, finance, medicine and so on. Each will have its own specific terminology and, again, its way of making sense and evaluating new information. It's quite common for these to clash with other internal expert discourses such as marketing. For example:

> In the legal world, disclaimers and terms and conditions comprise the most important information in the advertisement. So the legal team can't make sense of the marketing team's assessment that those lengthy T&Cs are off-putting to customers and should definitely be reduced to a footnote – and battles ensue.

'Terms of art' are words or phrases that mean something very precise within an expert group, and whose meaning is defined and controlled by the group itself. They may look like normal everyday words, but their meaning is tightly defined within the expert discourse. For example:

> In the UK the term 'advice' is highly regulated in the financial services market – only those with suitable qualifications can legally offer 'advice'. This technical meaning is very easy for customers and

others to miss – they'll hear this word in its everyday lay sense and potentially fail to understand important warnings given to them.

Interestingly, Schein (2004 p. 116) says that the assumptions beneath common words used with a special meaning become 'one of the deepest layers of that group's culture'. I tend to refer to them as 'swamp words' – they look solid on the surface, but they give way when someone tries to rely on them, as in the case of 'advice'.

'Compression' is also typical of expert discourses. For example:

> ➤ The discourse of finance and pensions features terms such as *'defer encashment'* and *'split beneficiary'*, where two or more expert terms (or an expert term and a 'swamp word') are combined, effectively baffling those outside. To explain these ideas in everyday language might take a few sentences, so experts see such compressed terms as elegant and precise. But they're typically very hard to understand outside that field of expertise.

Colloquial discourse

While you may not immediately recognize this as a discourse – it's just the way that people chat to each other in informal, social or family situations – it becomes noticeable when it appears to have a specific function within an organization's mix of discourses. The final example of 'discourse mixes' below will show what I mean by this.

Organizational 'fingerprints': different mixes of discourses

Sometimes it's clear that one or two of an organization's possible discourses are dominant or over-represented; this gives a clue as to the distribution of power across different functions and also points to overriding concerns and preoccupations across the organization.

Therefore, simply mapping the *dominant, less dominant* and *absent* discourses within an organization is a powerful analytic tool. It can help people understand conflicts in the organization and often points to the deeper underlying issues beneath persistent tensions. Insight into these is an important step towards dealing with them.

This is best explained by a few examples.

Example 4: Where's the customer?

A long-established financial services provider wanted to understand how to connect better with its customers, as it was concerned about a decline in its market position. There were also tensions and difficulties in agreeing marketing materials and information to be used with customers. So they asked for some help to see what was going on.

When we analysed samples of language from across the business, we saw that its internal language was dominated by three discourses:

- A *bureaucratic* discourse.

- Two *expert professional* discourses, specifically actuarial and legal.

- A preoccupation with *regulation and control*.

What *wasn't* seen? The company gave far less prominence than usual to the expert discourse of *marketing* (despite the best efforts of the marketing team), and it was almost totally devoid of everyday *colloquial* language. Both absences were quite unusual at the time, even for a large and long-established organization like this.

While bureaucratic discourse had been the norm in the sector, other companies in the same field had moved towards a less formal style, in line with broader cultural changes. In this company, though, it remained the unquestioned working discourse both internally and externally. Actuarial/technical/legal expert language was also very common, even in everyday exchanges and conversation within the organization.

An interesting quirk was that this company's internal discourse was also noticeably concerned with rules, regulation, procedures and control. This was visible in frequent – almost overwhelming – reference to 'the regulator', 'regulated' and 'the FSA' (the Financial Services Authority – at the time the UK regulator for financial service providers). The financial services industry was and is heavily regulated in the UK, but asking 'how could it be otherwise?' helped make it clear. We could compare their preoccupation with regulation with what we'd seen in many other financial organizations where such language was present, but far from dominant.

There was a broader but also dominant internal discourse of enforcement and control; the language was littered with examples of terms such as 'compliance', 'requirements', 'need', 'rules', 'approval', 'must', 'information', 'sign-off', 'disclosure' and 'contract'.

There were other small clues to the pervasive quality of the preoccupation with control, such as the 'Document Control Centre', which actually simply scanned documents – it might otherwise have been called something like the 'Document Scanning Centre'. The company also ran a 'letter approval process', which, given what it consisted of, might otherwise have been called a 'letter development process'.

What sense could we and the client team make of this? Historically, financial and actuarial technical expertise, and literacy in those expert discourses, had been top of the company's hierarchy. The increased strategic focus on the customer had begun to pose a threat to the authority of those locked into the technical expert discourse, and these tensions were playing out at the wrong level; that is, they were being fought in battles quite literally about how to communicate with customers – what language to use, and how much of it was needed. With this insight, the company was able to create a way forward. They helped everyone internally to move towards forms of language that reduced the exclusionary effects of the expert discourse, to create more closeness with customers (and better relationships with those in marketing and customer service), while also preserving accuracy and respect for the technical expertise.

Example 5: Managerial discourse goes on holiday

This client was a company trading in holidays, which are ethereal, transient and emotional experiences, albeit significant financial investments too, for customers. It was proud of its 'small company ethos' and was very keen to connect better emotionally with its target customers.

This sense of commitment to customers was very much present in interviews that we carried out with a set of leaders – note the intensified and emotional language:

> *That ethos of that small company is still there. That's really what we are... I still feel we are the good guys, in that actually, of course, we have to make money but we're genuinely desperate to give people good holidays, and I think we're better placed to do that than anyone else.*

However, in internal documents, the language of the company was dominated by a 'managerial' discourse, in which holidays were constructed as solid countable objects, like items on a shelf or in a warehouse:

> *The fact that we are curating our inventory basically is an extremely important differentiation point.*

> *... where we actually also control the entire distribution of the product into the marketplace and also distribute the product without having this facility.*

> *... so what we were doing is over-investing in the product and over-investing in the service.*

What did we make of it? Neither the 'emotional' nor the 'managerial' discourse is good or bad per se, but the danger we discussed with the client team is that if a technical, emotionless internal discourse (in which customers too were spoken about as objects in a process) were to become over-dominant, this could cause unnecessary problems by making it harder for the organization as a whole to think about customers in the way leadership wanted. It could also hinder good communication with them. Being aware of that tension was an important part of helping the leadership team think about its own culture and internal language, to help them meet their business objectives.

Example 6: Serious playfulness in a growing bank

This growing and highly successful British bank took pride in the culture of iconoclasm, playfulness and irreverence that it had at the start, and wanted to look closely at its own language as it grew. Looking at samples of its language some years ago, we could see that it had a particularly interesting discourse 'footprint' – one that gave far more prominence than usual to the non-expert discourse of everyday conversation and colloquialism.

▶ *Finance discourse*: unsurprisingly it did use this discourse, with terms such as 'the book', 'spend', 'risk pool', 'utilization', 'transactional behaviour'. These were quite standard for financial institutions at the time – although notice use of 'the book' to mean a set of customers. It's not always helpful, in our experience, to refer to real people in such a distancing way, even internally.

▶ *Marketing discourse*: the discourse showed typical patterns, including terms such as 'market penetration', 'proposition', 'product' (a credit card, or a loan was a 'product', for example) and 'the loans market'. Again, this was a familiar and standard expert discourse.

▶ *Everyday colloquial discourse*: a form of colloquial discourse was used internally, not just informally but in meetings and in PowerPoint presentations to discuss business plans, customer behaviour, etc. This was not at all typical at the time. This discourse used rather playful, quirky terms to refer to forms of customer behaviour. 'Jam-jarring' was the habit of saving money in several separate places or accounts for different purposes, such as for holidays, Christmas, large bills such as council tax and so on. 'What's in it for me?' was frequently used internal language that served to remind people to focus on the customer's needs, and not get distracted by other matters.

In the bank, iconoclasm, playfulness and irreverence were played out through switching and mixing, especially between expert and non-expert discourses. This clearly also supported one of the bank's stated aims in developing new services for its customers: 'a disregard for outdated conventions'. Breaking down boundaries, along with mixing and blurring discourses, was becoming something of a cultural trend at the time in the UK, also giving this internal discourse a contemporary and fresh feel.

Competing and incompatible discourses

We sometimes see clear and often bitter competition between two incompatible discourses – competing versions of 'common sense'. The question then is to ask whose version of 'common sense' prevails? And why? And how can the impasse be broken?

Here are two examples of this.

Example 7: Competing discourses: whose knowledge counts?

A significant US business-to-business (B2B) company had identified an important set of potential customers, but the huge diversity across this group meant it was proving hard to create a sales approach that made sense to all these target firms. At the time, there were two distinct tactics being proposed to solve this issue: one was embedded in the discourse of those at 'HQ' in New York, and one in the discourse of those in 'Field', based several thousand miles away across the US.

There was clearly a cultural rift between 'HQ' and 'Field', and this was posing a fundamental challenge for the organization and hampering the resolution of the problem concerning potential customers. They asked us to look at what might be going on and to help unblock the stalemate.

Analysing language drawn from both sites and covering formal and informal written materials, conversations and observations, we could see that the two professional groups – HQ and Field – were operating with two entirely different world views and discourses. They held fundamentally different assumptions about what matters or counts as valuable information, how one should make decisions, and therefore how best to persuade potential clients to engage with the organization's services.

Analysis of language from both sites suggested that each group was effectively 'saying' this:

The HQ discourse	The Field discourse
Large-scale data analysis is how we create useful knowledge – Field don't know the things we know about their clients.	*Conversations* with clients and our own colleagues are how we create useful knowledge – HQ don't know the things that we know about our clients.
It's our job to *control and manage* the Field and send them materials to use, based on our data analysis, to give clients what *we* know they need.	We must *work around* the material and controls that come from HQ, to give clients what *we* know they need.
Written items such as PowerPoint decks and written toolkits are how we communicate knowledge to the Field, and using them is how they should get important things done.	*Conversations* with clients and our own colleagues are how we get important things done.

Language sample: 'Mobile Solution emails were sent to marketing opted-in Program Managers [...]. The emails will drive clients to their Account Development Manager or the mobile landing page.'	Language sample: 'The people we talk to don't want to hear about how great our program is, they want to hear how it will make a difference in their world.'
So it's just common sense: Only *we* can see what really matters – because we operate at a higher and more general level than Field – we have the *data*.	No – it's just common sense: Only *we* can see what really matters – because we operate at a more real and specific level than HQ – we have the *experience*.

- The HQ discourse emphasized identifying patterns across the market, based on robust data and analytics – and handing these down to the 'Field' with instructions to use, embedded into what were genuinely designed to be useful 'aids' – PowerPoints, instructions/guides, template emails for clients, etc.

- The Field discourse emphasized understanding the distinct needs of individual clients, based on human conversation. They simply ignored the missives from HQ, or occasionally reworked them into their own discourse. And they carried on having tailored face-to-face and phone conversations with clients and prospects, as they'd always done.

The cultural rift went far deeper than terminology and into philosophical issues of how useful knowledge gets created. Each set of people, using quite different discourses and lines of logic, believed the other to be hopelessly and almost stubbornly misguided. There was huge waste and frustration, and a degree of resentment on both sides.

The company genuinely needed the best of both approaches – but when certain ways of thinking are deeply felt to be 'common sense' and these *compete*, it's hard to bring them together. For the company to get closer to this set of potential clients, 'HQ' and 'Field' first needed to *talk* with and *hear* each other and recognize that the other 'side' was not evil, or stupid, but was operating from a different world view. Mutual understanding had to be the way to trust and mutual respect – prerequisites for the work that would be needed to combine the genuine value in each approach.

We showed the leadership teams in *both* areas the findings of the discourse analysis and several conversations took place among us, leadership and team members at both sites. These didn't solve the problem overnight, but the recognition it produced started a process of productive action and shifts in understanding about what needed to be done.

Example 8: Two discourses competing to achieve a common objective

Some years ago, a UK public organization with a law-enforcement role within its remit was being required by government to become 'customer-focused' and this was causing turmoil within the organization. They asked us to become involved to help them understand why there was this turmoil and what being 'customer-focused' might mean for them culturally.

Analysis of a range of language samples, centring on constructions of 'customer focus', showed some distinct patterns: the language showed the organization was operating with one dominant discourse and one emerging, and in fact competing, discourse. *Crucially, these were aimed at exactly the same set of organizational objectives.*

We called these the 'coercive force'* and the 'facilitative' philosophies, respectively ('philosophies' sat rather better than 'discourses' with this client organization). They represented quite different ways of thinking about how to perform the law-enforcement arm of their work.

* Note that naming this discourse 'coercive' can now be read as a negative value judgement, but it was not intended to be so,

nor read that way by those then involved. That is, at the time, law enforcement in other spheres in the UK hadn't yet adopted a more 'facilitative' alternative approach to some types of crime. So 'coercive' was intended simply to be descriptive of that recognizable type of law-enforcement discourse.

The 'coercive force' philosophy: dominant	The 'facilitative' philosophy: emergent
The discourse entailed a rather muscular and energetic set of terms and phrases, bearing a clear relationship with other law-enforcement discourses of the day:	This discourse raised the possibility that people may need *help* if they're to comply; that the organization was confusing and hard to deal with; that people have different needs and that a one-size-fits-all and forceful approach was leading some to inadvertently fail to meet their obligations:
▷ compliance ▷ vs non-compliance ▷ enforcement ▷ officers ▷ 'the law says…' ▷ powers ▷ detection ▷ regime ▷ vigorously And especially: ▷ crack down ▷ tackle ▷ come down hard on ▷ pursue relentlessly	▷ information ▷ knowledge ▷ understanding ▷ fairness ▷ cooperation ▷ enabling ▷ facilitating ▷ support ▷ real-time ▷ efficient ▷ consistent ▷ sensible ▷ tailored ▷ reassurance ▷ relationship

The subtext here was:	The subtext here was:
'It's just obvious that this is how we need to behave to meet our objectives. And we need to do more of it too.'	'It's *not* obvious that what we've been doing is how we need to behave to meet our objectives. Maybe there's another way.'

While the coercive force discourse wasn't explicitly gendered, it was clear how masculine-coded it was (see next subsection on gendered language), especially with very frequent use of two powerful and somewhat violent 'shorthand' tokens for what the whole discourse advocated: 'crack down on' and 'tackle.'

This was underlined by the fact that, where scorn was directed at the facilitative discourse, it was commonly labelled as 'pink and fluffy.'

Both discourses were coherent but the coercive one, being far older, was rather more so. It's important to note that while certain teams or groups tended to be attached to one or other discourse, the discourses didn't map perfectly on to groups of people or individuals – they were *common resources*, available to anyone. In fact, in this case many people were using both discourses in a single conversation, sometimes in fact realizing that they were switching just as they spoke.

Gendered discourse

This brings us to the topic of gender. What's clear from our work is that an organization as a whole – or the typical patterning of its interactions and actions – can be 'gendered' and that this is reflected in and reinforced by its internal discourse. It won't be a shock to learn that, in our experience, most established organizations 'do' masculinity more than femininity. The historical roots of this run deep, despite recent changes in societal expectations and to some extent in norms of working patterns.

This is quite separate from issues of diversity in terms of headcount, special programmes, etc. – this is about the gendered-ness of the general milieu of discourse (assumptions, philosophy, common sense, etc.) in which all members of the organization find themselves working.

Let me explain why I say, '*do* being masculine/feminine'. There's much research and public debate about 'gendered' language – especially the debate about whether there's anything innate about it. Do men and women tend to talk in slightly different ways because of some trick of biology, or through socialization alone?

For the purposes of using language to shed light on organizational culture, we can most usefully think about gender as learned behaviour, almost as performance (Butler 1990). Gender as 'performative' is an established way of thinking about gender in many academic and other fields and is helpful here. Note that the idea of performative doesn't mean we 'pretend', but as very small children onwards we learn through socialization how to 'do being masculine' or 'do being feminine'. Of course, distinctive gendered codes of dress, posture, voice and language are historically and culturally specific (and are increasingly contested and in flux in today's emergent gender-fluid and non-binary discourses), but the performative principle still holds.

Organizations as cultures have established norms about how they act and speak, with associated habits and norms of thinking, problem analysis and presentation – and these can be seen as more or less gendered. So through these, organizations 'do' gender.

Some expressions of 'masculinity' we've observed in different organizations

▷ A global US-based corporate's default discourse was one of *thrusting macho talk, a linear and deeply rational and competitive masculinity.* For example, an initiative to attract more female customers was badged as 'Winning with Women' (and not, for example, 'Welcoming Women' or 'Including Women'). In another small but revealing example, a senior-level but informal working session was generally known as a 'shirtsleeves session', subtly reinforcing the sense of the masculine leadership norm.

▷ An international radical campaigning charity displayed *an 'angry young man' masculinity* – for example, 'F**k off' was used on campaign material (without the asterisks).

▷ A UK media agency's discourse was full of *muscular masculine idiom and slang.* Their 'New Joiners' manual contained, alongside the usual sporting metaphors ('Hit a home run'), many phrases like 'you get kicked in the nuts'; and 'fight for what you believe in'.

▷ A UK charity also *displayed a middle-class English masculinity – educated, quiet, polite and restrained.* This was not helpful to a campaigning charity where, in fact, people cared deeply about their cause; once we had shown them what they were habitually doing, they took steps to break away from this politeness and restraint, to great effect.

❖ Why these matter

Gendered discourse, as a way of thinking, sense-making and evaluating, has huge implications for gender inclusion (vs simple 'diversity' in terms of headcount) as well as for external relationships with customers, funders and others. What's more, gendered internal worlds tend to leak outwards – see the job description example below.

❖ What to look out for

Regardless of the innate/learned debate, in current Western culture we can simply observe that, in English, discourse that *reads as* 'feminine' or 'masculine' tends towards the features outlined below (see, for example, Tannen 1996):

'Feminine' discourse tends towards:

▷ Constructing symmetry, seeking connection.

▷ Conversationality (see Chapter 7).

▷ Displaying similarities and shared experiences – seeking similarity rather than difference.

▷ Including talking about 'troubles' – empathizing, offering parallel experiences.

▷ Unassertive strategies.

▷ Hedging (kind of, maybe, I think, perhaps...) and tentativeness.

▷ Tag questions (... don't you think?... isn't it?).

▷ *Offering* expertise (vs 'delivering' it).

▷ Offering knowledge and expertise, but in a way that ensures face-saving for the recipient – won't simply assert or lecture.

- Asking questions where necessary and useful to self/others (this is not seen as 'weak' or betraying lack of status).

- Collaborative talk.

- Co-creating; for example, finishing sentences for the other, filling in gaps, reading between the lines.

'Masculine' discourse tends towards:

- Ritual opposition and competition.

- Jokes – telling jokes, often against each other.

- Play fighting (banter), teasing, war metaphors, sporting metaphors.

- Debate – open opposition and open vying for status/position.

- Avoiding asking questions (questions betray lack of knowledge/status).

- *Delivering* expertise.

- Lecturing – displaying or 'delivering' expertise, independently of the recipient's response (see 'monologue' in Chapter 7).

- Rules and norms about how and what kind of information is delivered and valued; for example, dominance of numbers/graphs in PowerPoint slides (vs human voices, images or narrative).

- Problem-solving – responding to problems by offering solutions, not by listening/empathizing.

This is an enormous and often controversial subject and I'll necessarily just scratch the surface of it here. Here's one example, though, where the client organization's objectives were being foiled by almost imperceptible leakage of gender norms, despite a deliberate effort to avoid this. There's no particular value being attached here to one or other gendered discourse; their effects and contributions needs to be assessed in context. However, where an organization is actively trying to attract more women employees or customers, it's unlikely that a masculine-coded communication will be as effective as a more gender-neutral coding.

Example 9: Desperately seeking female engineers

A UK organization had been struggling to attract women into roles as field-based telecoms engineers, despite many initiatives and recruitment efforts. They asked us to analyse and re-draft a job description, part of a recruitment advertisement aimed at women, to see if and how it might be inadvertently skewed towards the masculine. They then carried out some small-scale research with women to compare the 'before' and 'after'.

When we analysed the job description, we saw several slightly gendered language features. Each was tiny and subtle, but cumulatively they built a distinct masculine cultural bias.

For example, the draft advertisement wanted someone who is:

> *'Open to new technology. Nothing too scary and we'll always support you, but you need to be comfortable using smart devices and ready to learn as new tools emerge.'*

The phrase 'nothing too scary' projects an assumption of anxiety in the reader. Would it say that if aimed at attracting men?

> *'Physically fit. You don't need to be a marathon runner, but will need to be fit enough to safely climb a telephone pole and carry a ladder.*

> *Prepared to roll up their sleeves. Working in the great outdoors on our network means getting your hands dirty from time to time.'*

A set of metaphors and idioms of manual labour were scattered through the job description, including: *will need to be fit enough to safely climb a telephone pole; prepared to roll up their sleeves; working in the great outdoors... getting your hands dirty* – (and others including *on the road* and *in your van*). Some checking against a 'corpus' – vast arrays of naturally occurring language – showed that, as we suspected, manual labour is still coded as masculine in today's wider culture. That is, in common usage these terms clearly refer to males and masculinity. Note that such coding is *a collective and evidenced cultural association* and operates regardless of the fact that there would be some women very happy to 'roll up their sleeves', and some men who would very much not want to.

We helped the organization to articulate what their intention had been in this language, then reworked that into less gender-biased text. Linguistic tweaking aimed to focus on the qualities required in an engineer, without introducing gender bias.

Original text – several features subtly coded the job as masculine:
- ...on the road
- ...in your van
- ...getting stuck in
- ...roll up their sleeves
- ...getting your hands dirty

Revised text – suggestions for a more gender-neutral version:
- I'm great at multi-tasking and managing my time
- I want a mix of working indoors and outdoors
- I'd love a job that keeps me fit and active, and I don't mind if it sometimes involves getting a bit dirty
- I love sorting something out for someone
- I'm good at just getting on with things

The job description was *intended* to signal that the company wants applicants who are:
- Active
- 'Can-do' in attitude
- Independent
- Able to get on with things
- Not hesitant or precious

But these and other key personal qualities are not inherently gendered, so more gender-neutral language was developed to describe them

Research involving 2,000 women tested the revised text against the original. When presented with the gender-inclusive version, women's interest in the role increased by more than 200%, with 60% stating this was because of the way it was written. The company has gone on to use this work across their recruitment and other parts of their gender equality and inclusion strategy.[2]

---

[2] www.openreach.com/news/new-research-reveals-hidden-bias-in-job-adverts-deters-50-of-female-applicants-for-roles-at-openreach/

It's likely that, beyond gender, other issues of diversity, equality and inclusion can similarly be investigated through discourse analysis. Examination of ethnically specific discourses, for example, hasn't been a significant part of my own consulting work. However, in the same way as for gender, it follows that an organization's ethnic, racial or other biases will be carried within, and perpetuated by, norms of language. The subtle but powerful nature of language norms as linked to implicit rules and assumptions of culture means that, without addressing this, true inclusion in ethnic or any other terms will inevitably be held back. I'm aware of at least one linguistic consultant working now in this area and I'm sure this field will grow.

'Professional' and 'unprofessional'

There's one form of discursive conflict that I've seen several times in organizational culture that deserves treating as a special case: that of 'professionalism'. Specifically, this is where one group of people in an organization dismisses another group, in extreme and often emotional terms, as 'unprofessional'. It's particularly problematic because it may well involve those in senior roles, and it engenders high levels of emotion.

It can be extraordinarily hard to unpick what's going on. However, if we consider what's entailed in the traditional 'professions' (medicine, law, architecture, surveying, accountancy, academia and so on) the roots of this phenomenon may become clearer.

Professional boundaries need to be protected because what's within them is both valuable and high-status. Each traditional profession is self-contained, a world of its own, removed from the everyday – and is a high-status world at that. Such professions are often defined *against* trade, managerial, technical, service, and manual occupations, which have usually been seen as of lesser status. Hence the desire for many areas of activity to 'professionalize', including less traditional areas, such as HR, market research and organizational management.

A 'profession' has its own canon and store of knowledge, its own training and induction processes, its own systems and institutions for the upholding of ethical and other standards. Being a recognized 'professional' brings legitimacy, status and power. It will typically entail extensive training beyond degree level; the acquisition of an extensive and complex canon of knowledge and methods of judgement; an ethical code of practice; agreed standards and accountability; swearing some oath to uphold these standards; certification or licensing; a professional association – and so on. As well as high status, professionals typically enjoy considerable autonomy, as professional associations often set rules and enforce discipline on themselves (see Fournier 1999).

So people with different professional backgrounds and training bring different unspoken priorities, judgements and habits of thought to their work.

One of the defining elements of a profession is having a *conceptual* knowledge system and an associated *abstract language*. So in HR, for example, an area of work that's increasingly 'professionalized', there's now a developed and abstracted language of 'competencies', 'talent pipeline', 'performance appraisals', 'workforce planning' and so on. Such abstractions – distinct from lay or everyday language around similar topics – are the working tools and boundary markers of a profession. It's clear that learning how to talk the talk is one of the necessary qualifications for many professions, and specialized talk is used in part to preserve the boundary around the profession, because not everyone can be allowed inside.

However, the problem we see in organizations is *not* at the level of this specialized vocabulary (although it can be annoying and alienating for one professional group to impose its own language on others) but the conflicts that arise from a deeper level of assumption and judgement about quality, moral value, and what's right and wrong.

Professionals learn early in their careers what 'counts' and what doesn't matter, what's right and good practice, what's wrong and bad or unethical practice, what good and bad quality look like and so on. These standards become utterly taken for granted and bundled into the category of 'being professional.' So anything that breaks these rules may be dismissed as 'shocking' and 'unprofessional' – *even if* it's legitimate within the professional standards of a different set of people, those standards being followed in a similarly unthinking and unconscious way. Each group may criticize and comment on the other but, within each domain, the decisions made and priorities set are constructed within their professional discourse as 'natural' and 'obvious' and 'right.' To each professional group, within its own world, making that decision or setting that priority is simply the correct and inevitable way to behave.

❖ Why this matters

Groups of 'professionals' in organizations are likely to have positions of significance and power. If there are competing sets of professional standards in play at a high level, but these are unconscious and not recognized, battles easily arise about 'surface' or operational issues, and frustration and intractable conflict arises.

❖ What to look out for

This kind of conflict is deeply felt – being 'professional' or 'unprofessional' is often constructed as a *moral* issue – so one might consider it as a possibility in situations where highly negative and highly emotional language is rife, but where people struggle to articulate further what the issue actually is. You'd see, for example, two or more groups competing for the label 'professional' in their own terms, effectively (but unconsciously) asserting the superiority of their differing models of value, quality and status.

> There might be a distinctly moral tone to the language used by each of these professional groups when 'shocked' by the other's 'unprofessional' behaviour. We'd watch out for the language of moral judgement and indignation ('correct', 'right', 'proper', 'shocking').

> Terms such as 'correct', 'right' and 'proper' also indicate the utterly taken for granted and inevitability of a professional world view – it can't be explained because it shouldn't need to be explained – it just *is*.

> In terms such as 'decency' and 'respect', too, one can hear the morality – and with a moral tone we know we're seeing something that really matters to those involved.

> At its worst, in such a situation, we've seen *ad hominem* dismissal (attacking the person rather than the argument) and derisive labelling. So conflicts between various 'we' and 'them' groups occur: we the fee-earners vs them in the back office; we the professional vs them the (shockingly) unprofessional; we the clinicians vs them the managers; we the professionally qualified vs them with 'non-jobs'.

Example 10: High-level conflict between professionals

In the midst of a significant organizational change within a public sector body – change in the operating model, the rewards system and in leadership, among other things – there had arisen significant conflict between the technical professional and the public administration groups. This ran from top to bottom of the formal organization and was causing difficulty across the board, even at the most senior levels.

We examined the language being used by both professional groups via conversations, documents and by observing meetings. There were many sources of distance and conflict, but it was clear that ownership of the term 'professional' and its implications was certainly at stake. Specifically, the organization had once been led exclusively by members of the relevant technical profession, and senior roles such as director of finance, head of HR and chief executive were generally filled by members of that profession. More recently those roles had been filled by people *without* the relevant 'technical professional' qualification, but who had expertise, experience and qualification in roles such as finance, HR and in leading public organizations. A clash of professional cultures rapidly developed.

Here are the unspoken 'truths' that were held within this particular professional conflict. These emerged from analysis of language, plus from an exploration of the issues with senior professionals in a series of conversations and workshops:

Traditional technical profession core beliefs	Public administration profession core beliefs
▷ 'Quality' is achieved by judgement, experience, 'art', local knowledge, apprenticeship.	▷ 'Quality' is achieved by processes, data, structures, routines, protocols, rules, standards of behaviour.
▷ Professional activity entails real-life exposure and meticulous in-person examination.	▷ Professional activity entails abstract, conceptual activity, and this can be applied remotely.

Data is useful but, in the final assessment, it's the judgement of the experienced professional that counts, even if it's not supported by the data.	Judgement is useful but, in the final assessment, data is everything. If it's not supported by data, it's 'just opinion' and doesn't count.

People in both professional groups needed some help to become aware of principles and beliefs they'd learned many years before and were now treating as 'obvious' and 'natural'. This helped to start different kinds of conversations, helped people understand the bitter disputes, and began to bridge the rifts.

Without recognizing their differences in these terms, and the potentially parallel legitimacy of both discourses, it had been impossible for those involved to have reasonable conversations about such things and to find common ground and mutual respect.

Stories

'Narrative' is widely recognized as central to human experience, and the role of stories in organizations as a way to make sense, coordinate effort and so on is also established. The narratives told and retold within organizations are in fact so useful that there are specialist agencies working primarily with stories, in leadership and organizational development. Here I'll cover them as one element within a wider mix of discourse features.

❖ Why these matter

Stories or narratives, and their elements such as *archetypal characters* are not always present in or relevant to a specific culture. But it's good to listen out for them; they can be revealing in themselves but can also help make sense of a wider set of clues about an organizational culture.

Small stories too – frequently repeated phrases, quotations or anecdotes – are often connected to bigger stories and may be being used as shorthand for a more fleshed-out cultural narrative.

Lastly, what I'm calling *fables* are frequently told stories that have a moral, or fill a culturally educational role – they serve to teach and remind people about 'how we do things around here'.

❖ What to look out for

Story forms, characters or archetypes

Think about the organization you work for or with. Are there stories that people tell or refer to again and again? Do these have a familiar shape to them – such as the 'hero's journey', a 'lost golden age', the 'good people's struggle against the wicked interloper'? Who are the heroes/villains/victims? How did the story begin? And how does it all end?

Example 11: The bad queen

We worked with a UK public sector organization that had been through a period of turmoil and change some years before, in which a senior leader overthrew the old way of doing things and introduced a radical (and very expensive) technology. The resulting machine-driven and less flexible approach to doing work previously carried out by skilled staff was not only creating discontent but was also proving to be remarkably ineffective. This narrative, and the characterization of its long-gone perpetrator, featured repeatedly in stories and conversations. It related to the past, but was still very much present, and sharing it as part of our reports led those involved to a deeper understanding of current issues and cultural problems stemming from it.

Example 12: The hero's journey/lost golden age

The classic hero's journey in which the protagonist sets out on a quest, encountering challenges along the way but ultimately prevailing, is a common one. An international charity for which I carried out research many years ago had 'we are the heroes' as its founding identity – a small group of special individuals who break convention, battle the enemy and save the day – deeply engrained in its culture. The creation myth and its founding figures remained prominent in everyday language, and a certain heroic energy still dominated the organization's discourse. These stories were told with nostalgia and a yearning for a time when the organization and all its people knew exactly what it was and what it was doing. They repeatedly expressed a desire to recapture the 'jaw-dropping' effect they once had; this was a key certainty they had from the past. Many years later, many people continued to present the organization as uniquely heroic – 'only a few people can do this work.' They'd failed to see that broader public culture had moved on, and that a more inclusive and less macho approach could now be more effective in engaging supporters and meeting its aims.

Example 13: 'It's okay, it's just a soap opera'

Soap opera is a very interesting form – unusually for a narrative, it doesn't have a beginning or end – it's all 'middle.' That is, in a long-running soap opera, events occur and characters may come and go, but essentially things stay the same over many years and episodes. We worked with a UK organization where most staff had been employed for decades, and had seen several changes of leadership in recent years. We noticed an episodic quality in how people talked about the past and the present – a familiar and relatively unemotional narrative: 'This happened because this person arrived, then that happened, then it all went back to normal. And then this other thing (another new leader) happened, and after *they* had gone, it went back again to how it had been.' So in the face of a new, serious and in fact *existential* threat to the organization, the unspoken narrative frame supported a passive sense of 'this too shall pass', which needed to be vigorously dismantled by the incoming leadership.

'Small stories' and fables

'Small stories' describing concrete, lived experiences may be heard (often focused on similar themes) across an organization. These stories have disproportionate power and significance – they can function to blame, justify, explain, complain and also to remind everyone of something. For example:

- ▶ 'Not walking past the spilt milk': A senior leader in a new and rapidly growing organization deliberately repeated several fables and 'small stories' to underline his intention and desire for the culture. This phrase about the milk was based in a real event and was now part of the organization's wider language – used by many to reinforce that consideration for colleagues and taking responsibility was part of 'how we do things around here'.

▶ 'Anti-social behaviour, such as stealing items from a communal fridge that are not yours to consume': We also saw milk appearing in a different way in small stories from within a relatively unhappy culture (in the UK we mostly like our tea with milk, and misbehaviour around the contents of the communal fridge can become a flash point!). In that culture, negative small stories were presented as documentary evidence of a dysfunctional 'big culture': transgressions like stealing items from the communal fridge being presented as emblematic of 'everything that's wrong with this organization'.

▶ 'We trust each other – it's a safe environment (nobody takes our milk from the fridge without asking!)': In the same organization, occasionally positive small stories were used to express and reinforce the team culture as being quite different from the 'big culture'.

Metaphor

What is metaphor?

'A metaphor is a figure of speech that describes an object or action in a way that isn't literally true but helps explain an idea or make a comparison.'

And a sustained metaphor is one that is:

'... carried through multiple sentences or even paragraphs. Because it is used and developed over a longer section of text, a sustained metaphor can be a powerful literary device that provides strong, vivid imagery in the reader's mind.'[3]

For example:

▶ The war metaphor that has long dominated the discourse of cancer is a sustained metaphor (although many people do now call for alternatives). So people will typically be said to 'fight' their

---

[3] www.grammarly.com/blog/metaphor/

disease, and perhaps sadly 'lose their battle'; as a society we are engaged in a 'war on cancer'.

Sustained metaphors are the most interesting and useful for organizational culture analysis. Within a broader look at the language of your organization, you might notice one or more metaphors being developed that are more specific or idiosyncratic to your culture. See 'What to look for' below for some examples.

❖ Why this matters

▷ Metaphor is hugely powerful – some say that metaphor is not only the way we structure language of all kinds, but also how we *think* (Lakoff and Johnson 1980).

▷ Metaphor is certainly a useful lens through which to think about organizations in general and there's a significant literature in this field (see, for example, Grant and Oswick 1996; Morgan 2006).

▷ Metaphors allow room for emotion and for inference – the opposite of spelling things out literally – so are especially sensitive for communicating or perpetuating organizational cultures.

A few cautions are needed, however:

▷ A dominant metaphor is useful in understanding an organizational culture, or aspects of it, but it's not the whole picture – some of its elements or 'entailments' will fit, but others may not. As Gareth Morgan puts it:

> '*Metaphors seize our attention, connect us with others, and simplify complex ideas. But they also trap us into a simplified way of thinking. At work, this means that the way we simplify our organizations determines how we can lead and embrace change.*
>
> *Metaphors are incredibly powerful. A good one grabs attention and helps people see through a shared set of eyes. But metaphors can also be a trap. They can obstruct our perspective, and in turn, limit our understanding of a situation, and confine our choices.*'[4]

---

[4] https://academy.nobl.io/gareth-morgan-organizational-metaphors/

▷ So, with a discourse lens, an organization's taken-for-granted metaphors effectively make some things sayable/obvious and other things not sayable/incomprehensible, but these profound effects are hardly noticeable to insiders.

▷ Finally, some metaphors have become so widely used that they're stripped of much of their metaphorical force – these are known as dead metaphors:

> 'A dead metaphor is a cliché that has become so commonplace that the imagery has lost its power.'[5]

I'd suggest that an example of a dead metaphor in common use in organizations is the formulation: 'We put the *xxx* (often "the customer") at the heart of everything we do.' Arguably, through overuse (and too often under-delivery of the promise) this metaphor no longer serves to carry much weight or meaning.

❖ What to look out for

'Organizing metaphors' are the way that the organization as imagined shows up in multiple language choices, sometimes more obviously than others. Here are a few short examples that we've seen in our consulting work:

▷ *We are a family.* A new organization had been formed from a much older established one and was about to break away entirely. Both they and the originating organization used a form of family metaphor – in this case the new organization was a bright rebellious teenager, about to set off into the world and excited for the future. The 'parent' organization looked on with admiration and pride, but also a little concern – they were brilliant, but could the kids remain safe in the outside world and actually do what they had to do?

▷ *We are 'family'.* A major airline consistently used a metaphor of the organization as a large and tight family. Quirks, criticisms and even bad behaviour were tolerated because 'they're one of ours'. Gaps between on-stage ('best behaviour please') and backstage language, especially about customers and the company's failings, were common. Tensions arose in many ways from this, including

---

[5] www.grammarly.com/blog/metaphor/

relationships with regular customers who tended to feel part of the family and therefore entitled to criticize the company publicly too, while those in the company resisted this vociferously.

▸ *We must defend the castle.* A public sector organization represented itself through its discourse as a heavily defended fortress, with all outside parties constructed linguistically as dangerous in some way. This idea became reproduced internally too, to the extent that a team with a crucial function was defended from anyone, inside or out, who wished to interact with it, by members of staff who had the official title of 'Gatekeeper'.

This next metaphor example shows a little more detail:

Example 14: We are at war

Legacy language within a team dealing with certain external stakeholders was coercive and confrontational – the metaphoric landscape in this case was the battlefield. This adversarial relationship had once been appropriate, but the world had changed and it was no longer serving the organization's purpose.

There was an embryonic 'journey' metaphor in use by some individual members of staff, offering a viable and potentially more effective alternative to build on. However, this needed to be recognized and supported in order for it to begin to spread. We worked with this organization to do this, building up the sense that there were alternatives to the aggressive discourse that *weren't* about being 'soft' or 'surrendering'.

The language samples below that we showed them within this process are a mix of their own language and our additions, to help them see the difference between the two metaphors:

War metaphor – in common use	Journey metaphor – a minority alternative
▸ They decimated our arguments	▸ They don't really want to come along with us
▸ We were right on target with that response	▸ Let's build some bridges

▷ Then they dropped their bombshell	▷ Look how far we got with them today
▷ We can't retreat from that position	▷ We're at a bit of a crossroads
▷ The other side said…	▷ There's light at the end of the tunnel on that settlement
▷ We're losing ground on this	
▷ I got caught in the crossfire	▷ We're rather off track
▷ Let's go for a quick hit	▷ We took a big step forward on this issue and now we're looking for the next one
▷ We crossed swords with their board	
▷ We seem to have come to a stalemate	▷ We seem to have come to a standstill
▷ We need to keep our powder dry	▷ We need to look at where we're going with this

Beyond these wide-ranging metaphors, metaphorical language can sometimes capture a particular moment, event or tension in an organization. For example:

▷ Working with an underperforming international corporate organization, we noticed frequent use of what we came to call 'metaphors of reversal' – terms such as 'full circle' and 'hokey-cokey'. It was clear that the present felt unstable and not to be trusted – the sense was that it will not only change again but it will *reverse*. As well as fatigue and cynicism about change, this appeared to express the frustration felt by the more ambitious; confidence in any decision is hard if can easily be turned around 'full circle'.

▷ In a different organization, the language analysis pointed strongly to a prevalent mental model of recent change as an *invasion* – an old-established group with one culture being invaded by a new 'ruling' set with a different culture. We were able to explore and extend this metaphor to help the leadership understand that it was the *mode* of invasion that was the focus of the negative emotional baggage accompanying the language. We introduced and discussed with them the idea of two kinds of invasion in English history: the Roman invasion – with its strategy of intermingling and integration with the local population; and the Norman Conquest – with its strategy of total dominance, separation and oppression. It was vital that they began to frame the formal change process in a way that acknowledged, but moved on from, the Norman Conquest model that they'd inadvertently built.

Finally, thinking metaphorically can also provide a useful frame for *addressing* a cultural issue or impasse:

▷ The same organization as in the last example had gone through a major change of leadership and mode of operating. The change had been necessary, but much organizational language now constructed a clear binary – the past was now to be seen as bad, and the now/future was to be seen as good. Unsurprisingly, many long-serving staff had found this difficult to accept, and even offensive. Beyond being careful not to reinforce binaries between past and future, bad and good, old and new in their own language, we suggested to leadership that they might use forms of metaphorical language to help the conversations in the organization move on to more productive territory.

▷ Seeking useful metaphors to represent a narrative of continuity; for example, 'building bridges' between then and now.

▷ Establishing a positive language of transition (vs the language of rupture or break); for example, 'metamorphosis', 'evolution', 'shift', 'conversion', 'development'.

We've covered a lot of ground in looking at linguistic clues to identity - who we think we are. These are big chunky ideas about marking internal groups and tribes, about signalling dominance and internal competition, about the stories and myths we tell ourselves, and the metaphors that help us make sense of who we are. Now we need to move on to 'them' out there, and the clues in language about who we really think they are.

Chapter 6
Culture question 2: Who are 'they' out there and what do we think of them?

This chapter, the second of our three concerning language features, focuses on how an organization's discourse constructs those outside of it – 'they' groups who are definitely 'not us'.

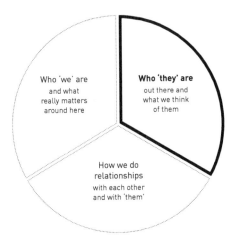

Who 'we' are
and what
really matters
around here

Who 'they' are
out there and
what we think
of them

How we do
relationships
with each other
and with 'them'

For a commercial organization, 'they' will mean customers, along with suppliers, regulators, investors, competitors and many others. For non-commercial organizations too, there's always a set of 'others' – healthcare providers have patients; tax authorities have taxpayers; governments have citizens and voters; charities have many (donors, fundraisers, regulators, governments and so on, as well as the recipients of care or help the charity aims to provide); local authorities have residents and elected members; universities have students, benefactors and so on. Note that we're less concerned at the moment with how the organization talks *to* outsiders such as customers, but more with the norms of talking *about* them internally.

Organizations need to have internal language to refer to and discuss external groups, and this forms a frequently used internal discourse. It's necessary for countless discussions, for example of strategy, communications, investment and so on. So it's a crucial window into the organization's culture. In this chapter I'll focus on how 'others' are constructed within such language – the ideas and assumptions contained within the language of the organization.

The chapter starts with a brief explanation of the terms 'construct' and 'constructing'. We then look at:

> *Who* features in the organization's external landscape.

> *How* they appear – names, labels, categories and implicit judgements.

> 'Subject positions'.

> Talking about 'customers'.

Although this chapter focuses on how people and groups *outside* the formal organizational boundary are represented in language, remember that the ideas here can also be applied to an organizational unit smaller than the whole. For every organization there will be multiple 'we' groups and multiple 'they' groups, even internally. So the marketing division as a 'we' will have several 'they' groups, such as legal and compliance, finance, etc. The European division 'we' will have a 'they', which is the US division, and so on.

'Constructing' those outside

Before going on to some specific linguistic ideas, I'll explain more about the process that in discourse analysis is called 'constructing'. Names, labels and categories are part of how we 'construct' all manner of things, including people, events and ideas. 'Constructing' means the way our language choices reflect and indeed reinforce our attitudes towards people, ideas or things, often unconsciously. Constructions are assumptions that are 'beamed out' holographically, and they're created in our language choices – *who/what* we talk about and *how* we do so.

Constructions of those *outside* the organizational boundary (however that's defined) are important *inside* it, because they have to stand in for that customer or other external people, groups or entities when they're not there. This means that, for example, some linguistic representation of a customer is effectively present in discussions of strategies for attracting them, or how to deal with issues concerning them. This especially matters because the way people and entities are constructed carries our judgements about them and affects decisions made about them. Those judgements may also 'leak' out and become visible to those people, sometimes with negative effect (see Chapter 7).

Who features in the organization's discourse?

We looked in Chapter 5 at who from *within* the organization (or division, team, etc.) features largely in its discourse; now we're looking at which *external* groups feature and don't feature in internal language.

❖ Why this matters

Simple presence or absence of people, groups or things 'out there' in everyday discourse gives a simple and useful starter clue to some important cultural assumptions and norms within an organization.

❖ What to look out for

Which external groups or entities feature large in an organization's internal talk? Who does it look like people care about enough to pay attention to (whether this is good or bad attention)? These may not always be the groups you imagine.

External groups or significant others could include:

▸ Customers or users – this is a crucial category for many organizations and deserves close attention

▸ Competitors

▸ Regulators

▸ Investors

▸ Supporters

▸ Suppliers

▸ Partners

▸ Donors

▸ The media

▸ Ministers/governments

▸ Celebrities

▸ Figures from the past (who are no longer 'us')

▸ and many more…

It's worth noticing whether any of these are clearly 'hot' or the focus of almost obsessive attention, and which groups or figures might you *expect* to see featured, yet are absent or barely there. For example:

Customers

▸ In an allegedly 'customer-focused' organization, customers hardly featured in anyone's language beyond the sales and marketing functions. However, beware – just because people *say* 'customers' a lot doesn't mean the organization is 'customer-focused', or even referring to real people.

Competitors

▸ Do competitors turn up much in language? It's not unknown for a company's culture to seem essentially blind to anything outside its own world. People in an organization I worked with referred to only a very small subset of competitors, and this was only in order to criticize and dismiss them. Sadly, this was linked with other evidence of a legacy pride that shaded into arrogance and was counterproductive for its current circumstances. I've also been told by a colleague about organizations where a narrow obsession with one or two competitors effectively encouraged 'copycat' products and allowed the organization to ignore disruptors who were aiming to grow into that company's space.

Regulators

▷ People within a particular UK financial services organization made constant reference to 'the regulator', not just within the relevant teams but right across different areas of the business. This proved to be emblematic of a broad culture involving some fear and a great deal of hyper-control (see Example 4).

▷ At another, the name of an international legal body was a constant refrain, invoked to justify all sorts of actions, and indeed lack of action. This body did have power over whether the organization was deemed to be successful in its remit or not, and could fine it for bad performance. But, even so, the organizational culture seemed obsessively gripped by fear, such that the needs of its own customers were neglected to the point of crisis.

Names, labels, categories and implicit judgements

One of the three cultural questions is 'who's out there, *and what do we think of them?*' This isn't about who those others *actually* are, but the way people in the organization *construct* them – working assumptions about them that are not necessarily conscious or articulated, nor 'true'. These include assumptions about their lives, their preferences and their motives. These constructions might vary between people or teams – a nurse may construct someone as an elderly patient, while the management team, oriented to their task of managing the hospital, might construct the same person as a 'service user' or even a 'bed-blocker'.

❖ Why this matters

Constructions of those outside the organization matter because:

▷ Relationships with external stakeholders clearly matter to business or organizational success, especially those with users or customers but also with investors, media, regulators, etc. And internal constructions of these groups affect relationships profoundly.

▷ The unique terms/shorthand/categories used internally to refer to relevant 'others' are so common and familiar internally that deep and important assumptions about them are easily hidden in plain sight. And these are often better brought to light and challenged, or at least debated.

So it's good to look for how an organization's language constructs important 'others', and what that suggests about its shared, unspoken cultural beliefs.

❖ What to look out for

Categories

These are systems for dividing up and thinking about the infinite array of phenomena in the world. They name certain things and omit others, rendering some things sayable and leaving gaps where other things have no language. They bring some things forward and push others to the back, and this has powerful consequences. For example:

▷ Several years ago there was a brief public outcry at a UK broadsheet newspaper headline: 'Mother of three poised to lead the BBC'. Commentators pointed out that, of all the categories this woman belonged to, 'mother of three' was the least relevant to her consideration for this powerful post and that it had no place on serious business news pages. She could easily have been referred to as 'Non-exec director at [*major international bank*]'. Meantime, commentators noted that both Bill Gates and Warren Buffett have each fathered three children, yet it's hard to imagine a headline about either of them that begins 'Father of three poised to...'.

The way in which categories are built and perpetuated is also very telling, yet usually unnoticed. They carry clues about the cultural view of what 'those' people are like 'out there'. And what we (really) think of them. That is, how outsiders are 'constructed' internally *may* run counter to overtly stated objectives and strategic intent.

For example, in my consulting work I've seen that:

▷ Customers may be projections of strong feelings: to be feared, or held in contempt, or depersonalized, or idolized, etc.

▶ Regulators may be enemies: feared too, but also derided and disdained.

▶ Competitors may be totally ignored, belittled or demonized.

The category is not the person, but categories in use every day in internal conversations, documents and meetings can feel remarkably real. They're only proxies and are subject to interpretation and filtering through the lens of the organization culture – and it's too easy to lose touch with the real thing. (Recognizing this has led some companies to bring 'real live' customers or users into the building to counteract this tendency.)

Here's why they matter so much:

▶ Categories and the ideas they carry are linked to decisions and actions – they have material effects. To use a rather crude example, the categories *the low-paid* vs *welfare benefit claimants* vs *slackers* all construct very different ideas about the rights and entitlements of certain people and will affect how they might be treated by wider society.

▶ Internal constructions of outsiders also leak out through *external* language – the cultural norms about 'what we think of them'. It's unlikely that an outsider will see overtly dismissive or problematic terms about them used in public discourse, but it's not unknown.

▶ Even if external people don't actually hear these labels, unconscious and unchallenged constructions in common use in an organization really matter. They don't just *reflect* attitudes, they *perpetuate* and *legitimize* them. And precisely because these terms are used so often, and because the implications of the language choices have become 'normal' and are easy to miss, they're important to include in analysis.

Names and labels

A shared internal shorthand and standard categories may be seen throughout an organization; including in the names of divisions or directorates as well as everyday conversation, and important assumptions and implicit judgements are often embedded into them. For example:

▶ *'The other side'* is a term very common in legal domains to refer to another set of lawyers and their client/s. What's entailed in this? It immediately establishes a metaphor of warfare – or at least of competitive sport – and therefore constructs and assumes an adversarial relationship.

▷ *'Prospects'* is a term used by many businesses about people who are not yet their customers, but who they see as potential customers.

What does the metaphor imply about the companies involved? Are they perhaps exploitative, scraping around in a metaphorical riverbed, like gold diggers, hoping to get rich?

What too does it imply about those 'prospects' themselves? Are they being seen as items just sitting and waiting to be scooped out of that metaphorical river, albeit precious items? What kind of relationship does this sound like?

▷ *'The big boys'* was a term used constantly by a small growing commercial organization to refer to their competitors (organizations from which, in fact, most of the staff had come). It was an essential part of a 'David and Goliath' narrative, important to people's sense of their organizational identity. As the company grew and became closer in size to 'the big boys', this identity became harder to sustain and was starting to hinder conversations and thinking about what needed to happen in its next stages. Allowing them to see this habit, and thus to find a way to move on from it, was an important outcome of our work with them.

Many familiar terms will be in use across an organization and it's worth contemplating their implications. The point is that we already have the intuitive skills to 'see' subtly embedded (and sometimes quite negative) implications, but we're usually too close to how these particular terms are used in our own organizations to notice them. Bringing them to awareness gives insight and choice about the embedded beliefs and attitudes, as well as about if, where and how you continue to use such terms.

It's an interesting exercise to collect all the names, labels and categories in common use in an organization and look carefully at them as a group. This can suggest patterns and implications, that haven't been obvious before - what this language is actually saying about those outsiders and where and how they feature in the organizational world. Looking also at the judgements and evaluations that are implied in how external actors are positioned is useful. Are they, for example, being positioned as passive recipients of the organization's actions? Are they being dismissed as something of a nuisance? Are they being idolized, or demonized? These implicit judgements and characterizations of 'them' blend into our third set of questions; that is, the nature of the relationships with others that are habitually constructed in language (see Chapter 7).

Subject positions

The idea of 'subject positions' is another concept in discourse analysis that's worth exploring, because it can be very helpful in looking at assumptions and norms within an organizational culture. A set of subject positions is the close or narrow set of categories offered to the reader by a text or discourse – positions and roles that they're invited to step into by the discourse. So we're also offered – or given – different positions by different discourses (see Jørgensen and Phillips 2002). For example:

- In a doctor-patient consultation, for example, the medical discourse clearly points to two subject positions – that of 'doctor' and 'patient' – and certain language and behaviour is culturally appropriate and inappropriate for the individuals occupying those positions in that moment.

- For someone else accompanying the patient, the medical discourse has a very limited set of subject positions: that person may well find themselves offered only something like 'carer', with accompanying norms and limitations of behaviour within the interaction, regardless of any material facts.

- This may or may not be problematic for that person, but it illustrates the way that a discourse can effectively constrain one's identity and action.

Subject positions constructed for outsiders by an organization's language may prove to be limited or skewed in a specific way. Although these are internal *ideas*, they affect myriad internal decisions and actions, including product development and communications, and how the organization engages externally.

Example 15: A restricting binary

Earlier, I described how a UK enforcement agency operated with a competing pair of discourses – the 'coercive force' and the 'facilitative' discourses. The coercive force discourse, the older and dominant of the two, set up just two simple subject positions for the people they dealt with: they could be either 'compliant' or 'non-compliant'. There were no other widely accepted or used categories. This pervasive duality was deeply embedded, not just into everyday operational language, but into the very structure of the organization as well. Citizens, it seemed, could only be good or bad, angels or devils, obedient or disobedient.

There was no room, for example, for those who were confused, or having life difficulties that made it hard for them to do what was required of them, or to do it on time. This had significant implications for how the organization was able to engage with people – the existing narrow approach took no account of nuance or difference among citizens, nor considered all their possible motives. This was proving unhelpful in an evolving cultural and political context.

The facilitation discourse said that we have to think differently about the messy real world of people 'out there'. Rather than the simple obedience vs disobedience binary, this idea helped the organization create several other possible subject positions for citizens, including being confused, or frightened, leading to a more sophisticated and nuanced engagement strategy.

Example 16: Not keeping up with customers

A food manufacturer I worked with many years ago operated then with two deeply engrained customer categories. Their plans, strategies and activities were organized around (at the time): those who 'cooked from scratch' and those who 'relied on convenience food'.

These subject positions and assumptions were leaking into prototype product and advertising ideas – but this binary was strongly resisted by women in focus groups. There was a gap – there was simply no public or marketing vocabulary for their cooking behaviour at the time.

When asked in research discussions, the women had to invent terms such as 'concocting' or 'practical cooking' to cover what they actually did (using certain prepared foods such as cook-in sauces, which were a new food product at the time, alongside fresh ingredients), to create acceptable and achievable family meals.

The company needed urgently to widen its repertoire of consumer categories and therefore subject positions in order to stay connected with the evolving lives and needs of those customers.

Example 17: Sidelining supporters

The campaigning NGO that I've mentioned before as being strongly heroic in its identity, typically constructed a limited set of subject positions for those outside through its internal and external discourse:

- ▶ *Potential admirers* of the brave actions of us, the activists.

- ▶ *Ignorant* – needing to be informed and persuaded about even the most basic general environmental issues.

- ▶ *Only able to deal with simplified and dramatic concepts* – 'ocean crime', 'climate enemies'.

- ▶ *Suppliers of funds* to support these extraordinary actions that *we* undertake.

Sadly, as with many organizations, this one had continued to construct such subject positions for outsiders long after those positions had become less relevant, after they had begun to create distance between it and important stakeholder groups.

Talking about 'customers'

There are two different ways we need to think about the use of the word 'customer' in an organization's discourse:

▶ 'Customers' in *commercial* contexts: people or entities who are targets of commercial activities and are being asked to buy goods and services, whether this market is business-to-consumer or business-to-business.

▶ 'Customers' in *non-commercial* contexts: the migration of the language of commerce and consumerism, and therefore the use of the term 'customer', into organizations and sectors where it hasn't traditionally featured, such as public services and education.

❖ Why this matters

Organizations and people within them need shorthand and common terms for key figures such as customers or users, to enable smooth operational running and management. However, when those common terms are oriented entirely around the organization's internal processes, this works against any effort to understand and treat those users as people, resulting in what people are inclined to experience as 'faceless corporates'.

Beyond this, if internal language is overtly or covertly disrespectful, or perverse in some other way, this too can get in the way of good effective business. In the examples below, there can be subtle leakage – the transfer of internal cultural attitudes, including those baked into internal customer constructions, out into externally facing materials and interactions.

❖ What to look out for

'Customers' in commercial contexts

You might think that commercial organizations would always create positive internal constructions of the customers on whom their livelihoods depend, and this is, of course, very often the case. However, I've seen apparently perverse, ambivalent or even negative constructions of customers within the internal language of some organizations we've worked with and, at the risk of focusing on the negative, it's interesting to show how discourse works in these cases. For example:

▶ The term 'punters' in British English is an informal and slightly derogatory way to refer to customers, and it would jar in many business contexts – but I've heard it used.

▶ There's also a tale – possibly apocryphal – about a major investment bank in the US where certain groups of clients were routinely referred to internally as 'muppets'.

Shown below are just a handful of the odd or unexpected ways in which customers have been constructed in our consulting projects: these are generally embedded into the organization's everyday discourse and have become utterly invisible to insiders. In each case, the casual but routine use of this language suggests something about the cultures of these organizations.

Customers defined entirely by their place in internal process/ system/priorities, or defined by the details of their contracts or transactions with the organization:

▶ *Policyholder (also PH), life assured, beneficiary, grantee, outflow customers, new to franchise, a bereavement claim* (referring to the person, not the claim).

▶ *Applicants, claimants, SBIs (single business identifiers), data subjects, post-Epsilon cases.*

Customers judged and evaluated:

▶ Customer = defined by the organization's loyalty scheme category, where the tier level stands in for the whole customer identity: *'he's Gold', 'Mr Gold', 'the Silvers', 'she's only a Bronze'* and *'they are Nons'* (people who are not part of the loyalty scheme). 'We have different policies for Golds and Silvers.' This identity obliterated all other differentiating characteristics and was a key element of discourse in a culture dominated by hierarchy and class.

▶ A US financial services organization had a division focused on selling services to other businesses ('business-to-business' or 'B2B'). One target market category was defined as 'middle market' and this idea governed much of its activity. As well as being inwardly oriented – those businesses were classified as a 'market' that's relevant to 'us' but not to 'them'. This term also proved in research to be patronizing to those being thus labelled. These companies were anything but 'middle' – many were very large, very successful and sometimes international businesses. Yet they were defined entirely in the context of the huge global client organization. This mismatch was not without consequence – it caused all sorts of issues in communicating well with people running those organizations, as potential customers.

▶ With another one of our clients, we came reluctantly to the conclusion that one of their underlying assumptions was that their customers were essentially rather stupid. How could we see this? In their language they constructed customers primarily as:

☐ Dumb victims – *'they don't know what they've been sold'* (even when they were sold the product by this company).

☐ Ignorant and slightly culpable – people who *don't understand financial matters* but who should (moral tone).

☐ Underlined by talk about the few unusual exceptions – customers who *'do know what they're talking about'*.

Customers being paid careless or casual disrespect:

▶ The *'punters'* and *'muppets'* examples at the start of this section.

▶ *'Clean cases'* or *'dirty cases'* = these were terms for *people*, the person being classified according to the complexity of their claim or case.

▶ The *'rate tart'*: a derogatory British term ('tart' is slang for prostitute) used in the past for customers who regularly changed their bank and other accounts, chasing better interest rates, introductory deals and so on. Thankfully (I believe) now fading out of use.

▶ Customers as a resource to be exploited – we aim to *'extract value'* from them.

Customers positioned as struggling and in need of us to rescue them:

▶ Customers (in this case, small businesses) positioned as not actively managing their businesses, or as downright struggling:

☐ 'Helping small business owners *finally* get a grip...'

☐ '... manage time, save money and *gain* financial control.'

Note that if small business owners don't already have a degree of 'grip' or 'financial control' they quickly fail, so this positioning was both nonsensical and slightly insulting.

Customers held in awe/better than us:

▶ Customers may be positioned as rather superior, and scary and better than us. Some organizations can become awe-struck by their customers – or at the *idea* of them – especially where these are upmarket and/or powerful target customers.

▶ This doesn't always lead to better interactions with them, as the organizational discourse is likely to be projecting anxiety or awe in its dealings with them, and this is rarely attractive.

Customers held responsible for creating their own problems – or even the company's problems:

▶ Blind and misguided: *'if they only knew us, they would love us'*.

▶ Manipulative: *'...and they know they're working the system'*.

▶ Customers *'don't understand our business'* (and should): staff saying competitor comparisons are irrelevant or wrong (because the companies are set up and funded differently). This is at odds with the customer's world, where it's a legitimate comparison – they have no interest in the underlying business models.

The variety of these apparently perverse, negative, ambivalent or even toxic projections about customers, and the regularity with which we've come across them in our consulting work, is striking. It may, of course, be a function of the fact that a good proportion of our work on organizational cultures has been prompted initially by difficulties in creating or maintaining good connections with customers.

'Customers' in non-commercial contexts

There has been a steady move in many Western cultures towards the marketization and consumerization of everyday life and discourse, and this brings associated language changes (and challenges) to previously non-commercial organizations. 'The customer' is, they may say, 'what we have to call them these days'.

'Customer' has become a term that's too high-level, compressed and indeed too common to be useful any more in many contexts. It carries so many different possibilities that people take different meanings from it, which may or may not be the ones intended.

For example, many educators in the UK strongly resist the idea of students as 'consumers', not because it's a change in lexicon, but specifically because of the meaning, ideology and consequences that they believe come with that change. So there may be rejection of the term 'customers' for use with students, for example, because of a resistance to the idea that they have *power* over suppliers (in this case, educators), or that it positions students as passive receivers of a product (where, in fact, they need to put active effort in themselves to benefit from the 'product').

However, teachers might take less issue with the idea of 'student as customer' as someone who should feel *respected* in their dealings with the institution and indeed individual teachers.

Example 18: What does being a customer mean?

Here's a very broad set of meanings that could come with 'being a customer' that we developed from publicly available discourse some years ago. At the time, a public sector client was struggling to become 'customer-focused', as it was obliged by central government to become. There was widespread dismissal of the idea internally on the grounds that 'they don't have a choice, so they're not customers'. Discussion around this list helped break an impasse, allowing for broader understanding of what else might come with 'being a customer' that was: a) within reach of the organization; and b) the right thing to do.

▶ *It's my choice to walk away.*

▶ *I have power over suppliers.*

▶ *Suppliers must fit in with my life.*

- *Things must make sense in my terms.*

- *I expect to feel respected.*

The organization in question firmly rejected the first two of these – and, in fact, citizens really *did* legally have to engage with this public body and had little power in that relationship. That fact had been used by some to dismiss the whole concept of being 'customer-focused', but breaking it out like this allowed conversations to happen about the other potential meanings in the list, and how these could be usefully implemented to the benefit of both organization and customer.

One more non-commercial example further shows the slippery nature of the term 'customer' and why it's important to look closely at *how* it's being used, and what work it's being employed to do.

Example 19: 'Customer' as code for 'trouble'

Within the language of a UK government delivery agency, the people one might think of as customers seemed to be invisible, or barely visible, external entities. They certainly weren't constructed as people or 'customers' in any of the senses in the list above. They were defined largely in terms of a range of labels drawn from internal systems and processes, such as 'Unique Business Identifier', reduced to 'UBI'.

However, some departments and job titles *looked like* they were concerned with entities called 'customers':

- There was the 'CRU' (Customer Relations Unit), a 'CMP' (Customer Management Pilot), and even 'Customer Champions'. So were there *some* official 'customers'?

On investigation, it emerged that these departments were *not* concerned with customers as a whole, but only with a specific subset.

In fact they were focused on *those who posed some kind of threat* to the organization's reputation or targets. That is, those called 'customers' were those making high-value claims, those making a lot of noise (via executive-level complaints, press complaints, etc.) and/or those holding high political power (MPs, union officials, other powerful 'stakeholder' groups). So those labelled 'customers' proved to be those constructed as troublemakers/threats, who were dangerous and needed to be pacified.

We learned from this and many other projects that whenever we see the term 'customer', it's worth taking a much closer look.

I've argued in this chapter that a shared internal notion of who and what is 'out there' is a central part of an organization's culture. This has meant looking at the external groups or entities that feature in the internal language of the organization, and at assumptions about those groups that are normalised through habitual language - especially via categories, names and labels that contain implied judgements. Next, we'll move on to the habits of language that offer insight into an organization's cultural norms about internal and external relationships.

Chapter 7

Culture question 3: How do we 'do' relationships with each other and with 'them' out there?

So far I've looked at questions of *identity* – what the organization's characteristic patterns of language suggest it assumes both about itself and about those outside. Now let's look at the *relationships* that are assumed and constructed in its language. How do we 'do' relationships through language – with each other, and with those 'out there'?

In Chapter 2, I explained that the slightly odd 'doing relationships' expression serves to remind us that we're interested in the way people in the organization or group go *about interacting with and relating to* each other and to 'them', not in what that relationship 'is'. Is there, for example, a shared habit in interaction of assuming a position of superiority? Or perhaps it's culturally the right thing to offer a degree of informality and intimacy as a default position. And so on.

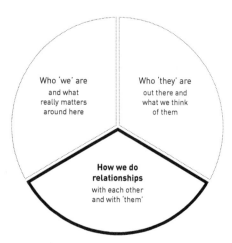

Relationships matter inside and outside organizations, for many and obvious reasons, and these internal habits and assumptions will shape those that are actually formed with colleagues, teams, divisions and with others operating externally. To reiterate, these habits are subtle, engrained and can be hard to articulate from inside, but they do have consequences.

As we've seen, potential relationships are implied in how we speak *about* ourselves and *about* others. But they're enacted, strengthened or challenged in everyday interactions – how we speak *to* and *with* those others. And, of course, I'm using 'speak' and 'interactions' to include spoken and written language of all kinds (covering images too), including that found in emails, reports, PowerPoint presentations, board papers and more. Patterns in relationship norms and interactional norms tend to involve issues of power and status, cooperation and respect – as you might expect. There are some useful linguistic principles and frameworks that can suggest what's going on in these terms, as part of a look at an organization's culture.

These are linguistic features associated with:

- Power and agency
- Formality and 'properness'
- Distance and closeness
- Politeness and 'facework'

Power and agency

The assumptions we make about who holds the power to act and who is to be acted upon can be read or at least glimpsed in everyday habitual language. This is the default stance that's habitually taken with regard to others and is relevant to internal relationships and in relation to those outside its formal boundaries.

Internal power and status patterns may be reproduced with those outside, or not, but it's helpful to be aware of them. So a marked 'parent-child' internal culture may also be expressed externally in some form in the organization's dealings with partners, customers, etc.

❖ Why this matters

As social beings, power and status are often important to us, so we have lots of ways to signal this. But this is obviously especially important in most organizations, where relative position and decision-making authority are also associated with status and material rewards. It matters, too, to government law enforcement and other public sector organizations that have, and wish to exert, formal power. And power matters to those trying to persuade or compel others to behave in a certain way, whether for commercial or non-commercial reasons.

My observation is that, in general, large organizations and long-established organizations assume power over others, consciously or otherwise. This can be a habit that's hard to break, even if it has become counterproductive. But why does it matter? Shifts in wider cultural norms over time mean that heavy-handedness or assumed superiority, even if implicit or unconscious, becomes an anachronism or even a liability.

- There has been a well-observed 'decline of deference' in many Western cultures, such that collectively people no longer have the same respect for large institutions such as banks, governments or other traditional establishments as was once the case.

- The marketization of domains such as education, too, may shift old power structures. If a student is constructed as a 'customer', they may well expect or even demand quite different things from teachers and institutions than was the case for earlier generations.

- 'Partnership working' is now increasingly common in public sector, healthcare, social services, etc. – or at least is advocated. In practice, this will be fundamentally affected by assumed power superiority that is played out in meetings, conversations and other apparently partnership activities.

❖ What to look out for

There are many different ways to signal relative power/authority in language, and most of them are (in English at least) quite subtle – they're hard to point to, but their effect is felt, especially by those with less actual or assumed power.

This isn't about *conscious* processing – subconsciously, as a recipient, we're generally aware of the actions people or organizations are performing with their language. We feel it when we're being subtly complimented, helped, treated as intelligent, flattered and liked – and equally when being insulted, treated as 'other', put down, diminished and so on. We sense these things, even if we can't work out exactly why we feel that way. An example may help:

Example 20: Who's in charge here?

This huge aid agency's stated intent was to attribute power and agency wherever possible to people and groups with whom it worked and provided aid. However, we saw a pattern, through large-scale analysis of its external communications, where the NGO persistently positioned itself in grammatical structures as acting on recipients of aid, not working with them. It showed mainly in two patterns:

▶ Active/passive constructions: using large-scale quantitative linguistic analysis, we could see that the NGO was positioning itself as engaged in physical constructive processes, involving effort, and having tangible results: it *'supported, reached, provided, worked, distributed, changed'*. In the same data, local partners were largely positioned as reacting to external pressures: they *'needed, benefited, fled, got sick, didn't understand'* and so on.

▶ Transitivity: who does what to whom, who is subject and who is object. This different analysis showed the same trait; for example, stories about local people trading with developed nations would typically be expressed as *'we buy x from them'* and not as *'they sell x to us'*. This is such a small difference, but as a language habit multiplied over thousands of texts, it subtly signalled the attribution of agency and was thus cumulatively working against the NGO's stated intent.

Here's a selection of the micro-features in language that contribute to those kinds of feelings around assumed agency and power:

- ▷ Verb choice: *force* or *drive* vs *encourage, invite* or *request.*

- ▷ Deontic modality: a linguistic term for the class of verbs and forms that contain within them some sense of obligation or a view of how things ought to be; seen in examples such as you *must, should, never, always.*

- ▷ Transitivity: in the example above, who tends to act and who tends to be acted upon can be inferred from how sentences are structured.

- ▷ Spatial metaphors of position: especially *up/down, above/below, ahead of/behind.*

- ▷ Monologue vs dialogue: speaking *at* vs speaking *with.*

- ▷ Politeness and 'face-saving' language: the greater my power, the less I need to be 'polite' (although I may still choose to be).

The examples that follow show how some of these features play out:

Example 21: Doctor power: the UK's medical profession

In the UK's National Health Service, a recognized power imbalance, often labelled paternalism, remains prevalent. There have been many attempts to level out power imbalances between doctors and patients, but few seem to have had any effect.

In fact, aspects of the language used in these attempts seem to subtly underline the existing power structures, even when trying to signal the opposite. For example, many initiatives talk about 'empowering' or 'including' patients – but assuming the right to give power away to others (to 'empower' them) or being in position to 'include' or exclude them are, of course, positions of power.

Example 22: Parent-child dynamics: a local authority

The culture of a UK organization with which we worked revolved around a pervasive parent-child dynamic, easy to see in its language. Parent-child bossiness/ submissiveness was in evidence at all levels, even in notices on walls.

- ▶ A poster suggesting people bring a reusable water bottle to work then reminds them to 'keep it clean and germ-free.'

- ▶ Posters on the wall of an 'innovation space' exhorted users to 'think freely..', but an equally large notice told them exactly how they must leave the room – clean walls, lights off, chairs replaced, pens, etc. 'tidied away' and so on.

- ▶ The hand dryers in the on-site bathrooms had a notice above them giving instructions for their use – something I'd never seen before. The dryers were a very common type and would have needed no introduction, let alone instructions for use. So posting this notice seemed to be another piece of data that expressed the cultural subtext, which we eventually captured as something like 'everyone will behave like a child unless I tell them not to or make sure they can't.'

Example 23: Levelling-up power? A US global company

An incoming CEO announced that those known as 'staff' or 'employees' should now be known across the global organization as 'colleagues' – which looked like a move to even out power hierarchies, even if in a small way. Interestingly, though, at the same time, he also mandated that email signature lines be used, with names, locations and job roles, thus re-enabling the expression of status.

Example 24: Thwarted authority: a major UK transport provider

This company needed to deal with a large backlog of customer complaints, many of them having been directed to the chief executive's office. The team responsible for handling complaints had devised a single 'holding' email that could be sent en masse to large numbers of complainants as a temporary measure. The internal name for this campaign was telling. It was called the 'Big Kill' email. Although this name was, of course, intended only as internal shorthand, it could be seen as betraying something of the impatience and annoyance felt internally at having to deal with this problem, and as a covert reassertion of authority.

Formality and 'properness'

Typically, senior leaders or those who are not in communications/marketing functions often feel it's just 'not right' to address customers or others in an informal way. In older organizations this often crystallizes around a sense of how we 'ought' to sound – especially when the desire is to be professional, authoritative, dignified and proper. It's hard to persuade people to let go of language they see as 'right' or 'correct' or 'professional' – there are clearly deep-rooted learned moral judgements in play here. Many people who now hold senior positions in such organizations would have absorbed certain rules at school and may strongly resist alternatives that they see as ungrammatical or sloppy. Or they fear that the only alternative to old-school formality is the unthinkable alternative of 'text-speak', slang and emojis.

The norms around organizational language have already changed – the standard in many Western cultures is now less formal and more 'democratic' than even ten years ago, and we see this across private companies, government institutions and the third sector.

❖ Why this matters

Just as it needs to keep its packaging or logo updated, a company or brand must keep its language updated, *at a level appropriate to its other values*, in order to remain in its position, or it can begin to look old and faded. It's also clear that the idea of the 'employer brand' is hugely important as the competition for talented young workers increases.

Thus, organizational communications using a formal old-school voice *externally* now risk creating distance between themselves and the outside world. Widespread use of it *internally* risks sustaining a working environment that feels stagnant and that alienates newcomers. New joiners, even the younger ones, rapidly adopt the style they see and hear around them, especially in written texts, absorbing 'how we seem to write around here'. This often results in employees using archaic and stiff language – and the formality is perpetuated.

The other effect of formal language is to imply a degree of superiority. As the role and importance of traditional authority structures declines (police, government, state, medicine, etc.), communications need to establish (or at least mimic) a more 'equal' relationship with readers – and informal conversational discourse characteristically entails a temporary suspension of status differences.

Choice of language style, often entirely habitual and unconscious, has a significant effect on interactions with outsiders, and improving style and communication is often the role of communications experts and copywriters. However, there's clear evidence of a 'drag' effect of internal culture on such interactions – for example, we know that it can be hard for agencies and internal teams to get senior sign-off for communications that have been developed primarily with the user or customer in mind.

As well as some clear arguments for reducing an organization's use of 'formal' language, I'd definitely regard its presence as a clue to a set of cultural beliefs that are keeping it in place and policing it. Formal language tells us something about 'who we are'; for example, an unspoken belief that 'we must remain dignified, proper and professional at all costs and regardless of the external world'. So insistence on formality is an interesting observation to consider in analysing an organization's culture, and while this is treated here as a topic within 'how we do relationships', it's just as relevant to the first cultural question about 'who we are'.

Here's an example that shows the effect that even a small difference in formality levels can have on both a construction of the customer and the sense of self that the organization projects in its choice of language:

Example 25: Doing relationships in different ways – airline safety videos

---

Here are extracts from transcripts of the mandatory passenger safety instruction videos being used at one point by two different airlines. This is a good example of the comparative method in discourse analysis – the same (regulated) content is expanded in language by the two organizations, who insert into it their different ideas of who they are, and the relationships they assume or desire with their customers.

Even from these brief extracts, we get a sense of who each airline thinks they 'are'.

Airline A

> *Your oxygen mask is behind the panel just above your head. If the cabin air system should fail, this will be released. Stay in your seat and pull the mask towards you to open your supply. Please note that the bag does not inflate. Place it over your mouth and nose and adjust the band to secure it, then breathe normally. Do make sure your own mask is correctly fitted before helping anyone else.*

Airline A's version suggests it's a company that constructs itself as 'respectable', formal, posh and somewhat old-school. For example, it uses strictly grammatically correct forms such as 'if the cabin air system should fail' (vs colloquial 'if the cabin air system fails'); and the passive 'correctly fitted' (vs the 'make sure it fits' of the second airline). The language might be read as positioning the airline as a little superior to the customer – 'ordinary' people can certainly read and understand this kind of language, but most are unlikely to produce it themselves.

Airline B

> *If oxygen masks drop, keep your seatbelt on and pull the tag or the mask down to turn on the oxygen. The bag might not inflate but oxygen will be flowing. Put the mask over your mouth and nose and adjust the straps around your head to make sure it fits. Take your mask first, before helping anyone else with theirs.*

Airline B's version is a little shorter, uses simpler vocabulary, such as 'drop', and 'put' (vs 'place it'). Importantly, it also uses simpler sentence constructions that are closer to the structures of spoken language than to written ones. It subtly suggests itself as closer to the passenger – conversing with them rather than announcing at them, and definitely not positioning itself as better than them. This airline cannot fully flex the humour it's known for in the safety video script, but its language is as clear, straightforward, informal and contemporary as it could be in this context.

❖ What to look out for

In English, many of the features that we'd classify as 'doing' *formality* in language cross over with those that construct a sense of *distance* and will be covered in the next section.

However, I'll cover one important linguistic feature here, as it's closely connected with the idea of formality, perceptions of class and of 'properness' in English; that is, the difference between spoken and written lexicon, and the lasting associations these have in English with social class, education and therefore power.

A significant element in formal vs less formal language is the choice of words. The English vocabulary is huge, and we can often make fine distinctions with our choices. However, an extremely significant choice for our purposes is that between words originating in the early medieval

English that was in use at the time of the Anglo-Saxons, and words stemming from the old French that arrived with the Norman Conquest of England of 1066. Here I'm greatly indebted to Abi Searle-Jones of the consultancy *and/or/if*, and with her permission I've edited and quoted liberally from her personal notes to me on this subject:

The Norman Conquest was the biggest language shift in English history and shaped the English language more than anything else. Before then we all pretty much spoke what's now known as 'Old English' or 'Early Medieval English'. That was a Germanic language, and all our basic 'gut' words come from it, such as arm, cow or eat (and many words for 'stab'!).

When the Normans arrived, they brought with them Norman French, which was a Latinate language; that is, rooted in Latin. This was definitely a written language, as they used it for legislation, record-keeping, taxation, etc.

So, while most people carried on running around *speaking* the old version of English, those who were *writing* were doing so in Norman French.

A thousand years later we still do the same thing; English speakers are all effectively bilingual. We naturally use 'older' English words while *talking*, and often fall into Norman French-derived vocabulary when *writing*.

You can see this most clearly in the thousands of word pairs we have that offer a choice – we can use an older English term or a word derived from a French/Latin root:

▶ Heading home tonight, I may see a sign that says 'roadworks will commence on 15 October', but when I arrive, I'm not likely to say to my son, 'Have you commenced your homework?' I'm far more likely to ask him, 'Have you begun your homework?'

▶ Similarly, I may say he can play on the iPad 'once you've eaten dinner', but not 'once you've consumed dinner'.

▶ 'Begin' and 'eat' are from Old English; 'commence' and 'consume' are Latinate/French.

This earlier English vocabulary is simple and very powerful; Churchill, the master of the English language, used words drawn from it in most of his speeches:

> ▶ His famous 'we will fight them on the beaches' speech is entirely free of Latinate vocabulary, apart from the word 'surrender'. He said, 'We will fight them on the landing grounds' rather than, 'We will engage with the opponent on the zones of disembarkation'.

You can also hear the *class* difference in these two different vocabularies. Norman French is the 'posher' language, the language of aristocracy. (It seems significant that the words the British monarch speaks to pass legislation are still in French.)

Differences in *education* are encoded in this vocabulary split too. As children learning English, we tend to learn the more basic, Old English-derived vocabulary first, learning our Latinate vocabulary later in life. This latter vocabulary increases with education and with engagement in a professional life involving a lot of writing, which many people do not become involved in.

A few decades ago this division between informal=spoken and formal=written started to break down. As it did, large organizations, even government departments and 'traditional' organizations such as banks, started to move towards a more conversational tone, and a simpler older English vocabulary. For many this now applies to both external and internal language.

In this environment, organizations that continue to use a traditional written tone begin to look old-fashioned and bureaucratic, a little superior, and out of step with the language culture.

So what's the value of this for analysing organizational culture? It's significant for our purposes that the implied class and education divisions carried in the two sets of vocabulary continue:

> ▶ Because of this, a subtle but effective way to project a sense of superiority and power over others is to use this more 'educated' vocabulary, especially in some contexts. For example, the negative

effects of formality in letters directed to customers or citizens are well known; it can result in people feeling excluded or patronized, becoming resentful, or even ignoring important communications altogether.

▷ Conversely, individuals can, if they choose to, reduce power and status differences a little by using more accessible vocabulary in both speech and in writing, and this also applies to organizations as a whole.

Distance and closeness

There are two useful linguistic dimensions through which a sense of distance or closeness can be constructed by language: whether or not the writer or speaker seems *present* in the language, and whether they seem to be talking *at* the other person/entity involved or *with them*.

These are relevant to considering organizational norms and habits around 'doing relationships'. For example, is the habit of an organizational group to refer to matters indirectly and through abstractions, or to use language that makes it clear who and what's involved? Is the habit to 'deliver' a monologue, or use language to create some kind of dialogue? What these options look like, and their relevance, will be made clearer below.

Being present or absent in the language: passives and nominalizations

In this section we'll look at two ways that different forms of language can seem to make their producer distant and/or not responsible for the language or its implications. Technically, these are the *passive* voice and the use of *nominalizations*, and in practice these are often found together, effectively hiding the agents or actors; that is, the people and things involved.

❖ Why this matters

Passive constructions are strongly associated with 'scientific' discourse, where they create a sense that scientists are dispassionate and their findings are objective. They do this because agentless passives remove the agents (people) from the language altogether. In fact, the most active agent in scientific discourse is often inanimate, in the form of the *data*, which often 'show' or 'suggest' things, as if all by themselves.

Passive forms impose a greater cognitive load on the reader, slowing down comprehension and often needing a higher reading age. This is not helped by the fact that they're often combined with Latinate vocabulary. For example, '*modifications to domestic arrangements must be disclosed*' is far more demanding to decipher than '*you must tell us if you change anything about where you live and who you live with*'.

In organizations, extensive use of the passive tends to make writing sound more formal and objective. But it also creates and sustains distance between people, between teams, between leadership and staff, or between other groups. Passives hide *who* is doing/saying/deciding something and may also fail to state to whom the thing is being done/said, etc. For example, '*redundancies will be kept to a minimum*' says virtually nothing. Passive forms are therefore often unhelpful and may typify what's now felt as 'faceless bureaucracy'.

But, more importantly for our investigation of culture, in airbrushing out the actors, passives *obscure responsibility and accountability*. Decisions can therefore be dissociated from the decision-makers, *and* from their consequences, *and* from those who bear those consequences. (Possibly, for this reason, passives are also much loved by politicians and governments.)

❖ What to look out for

Passive constructions focus on the *result* of an action, or the *thing/person being acted upon*, rather than the person *performing* the action. For example, 'the dog was examined by the vet' (passive) vs 'the vet examined the dog' (active).

Agentless passives go one step further and leave out the person or thing performing the action altogether: 'the dog was examined', or even 'veterinary examination of the dog was undertaken'.

A simple test for an agentless passive is to mentally try adding an active agent to the sentence by tacking on 'by monkeys' or, if you prefer, 'by zombies' (with thanks again to Abi Searle-Jones). If it then makes (some) sense, what you started with is an agentless passive. If not, it's not.

> ▷ So, just for fun, this is an agentless passive: 'The dog was examined – *by monkeys*'

> ▷ But this is not: 'The vet examined the dog – *by monkeys*'

Nominalization is another distancing device. This is where a process is turned into a thing or noun; for example, *government, globalization, inclusion, improvement*. And, indeed, *organization* (which, it can be argued, is a process and not a solid thing – see Preface). In English, words that end in the following letters: -ion, -ment, -nce, are often nominalizations. Just like the word nominalization itself, of course!

Nominalizations often coincide with a Latinate vocabulary and with the passive voice – so switching to the active version of a passive/nominalized sentence *and* seeking the simpler, older English word is often recommended for clarity. The resulting sentence or phrase may or may not be shorter but is always clearer, and, importantly, puts back the agents and actors. We know who's doing what to, with, or for whom. For example:

> ▷ Acknowledgement of applications will be sent. ✘

> ▷ When you have filled in the form and sent it to us, we will confirm that we have received it. ✓

> ▷ An investigation will be carried out… ✘

> ▷ We will look into…✓

Nominalizations, Latinate vocabulary and passives are characteristic of a 'bureaucratic' discourse, and are heavily engrained in the working discourses of many organizations, at least in written forms. However, they do harm to many attempts to 'engage' staff or customers. For example, we see this voice, unfortunately, rather often in high-level announcements and policies, for example from HR, and sometimes in senior-level all-staff communications.

Talking at or talking with: monologue and dialogue

Another useful distinction in language is between *monologue* and *dialogue* – the difference between talking *at* someone and talking *with* someone. This dimension has a clear role in constructing closeness in a relationship, or underlining distance within it, and therefore in setting the tone of an exchange or a relationship. This is therefore important enough to treat separately from the passive, etc. in the context of cultural assumptions about relationships.

> ▷ Monologue (declaring, stating) – is one-way; I tell, you listen; like old-school authority. It can sound self-important and deaf to the

needs or priorities of others. *It constructs a sense of the speaker/writer being in charge.* A letter headed 'Important Information' and that makes no attempt to address the reader, or anticipate the reader's response, is highly likely to be monologic.

▷ Dialogue (sometimes 'conversationality') – is closer to actual, real conversation. It uses language that conjures a sense of *you*, the reader, as you read. It gives 'you' a presence in the 'conversation', even if it's technically one-way material such as an advertisement, email or a letter. *So it's more likely to construct a sense of equality and openness in relationships.* As a small example of a dialogic approach, one famous airline doesn't print 'Menu' on the front of its in-flight menu – the cover simply says 'Drink?'

❖ Why this matters

Unsurprisingly, the monologue/dialogue dimension is especially relevant to the outward-facing language used by an organization; for example, in interactions with customers and in materials like advertising and customer emails. These are a major means by which internal cultural attitudes leak out to the outside world. If a company says it wants to build relationships with customers but then simply shouts things at them, this desired outcome is unlikely to be realized.

However, an organizational habit of monologue or dialogue is also a barometer for cultural norms about the other aspects of culture I've discussed already – the shared sense of self, or who we think we are (or perhaps want be) and our stance vis-à-vis all other groups.

❖ What to look out for

What are the characteristics of a 'monologic' form of language? A 'monologic' text often feels designed to be read or even studied and is awkward to speak out loud (so a good test of its opposite, conversationality, is to read it out loud). It may well use long sentences and lots of subordinate clauses, and in doing so creates a high cognitive load – it takes little account of how you, the reader, may be receiving it.

Monologue will give a sense that it's declaring, stating, asserting, telling, announcing without caveats (it *is* vs it *could* be). There will be an *absence* of 'hedging' – expressions such as *perhaps, possibly, sometimes, generally* that express a degree of hesitation or indecision about what's being said.

It will sound like an announcement from top-down authority, the great speaking to the lesser; it can sound parent-child (*don't talk back, just listen*) or head teacher-pupil.

It may also be all about *us*; you just need to listen and be impressed.

What are the characteristics of a 'dialogic' or 'conversational' form of language? Note first that dialogic or 'conversational' discourse is entirely possible in one-way contexts such as written material for a mass audience – the co-conversant doesn't have to be present. And also note that conversationality doesn't mean using slang, or 'text-speak', or embracing slackness in grammar. It simply means using structures common in spoken language within written material.

A 'dialogic' text will sound 'conversational', that is, informal yet with some structure, like peer-to-peer interaction; it also gives a sense of adult–adult interaction.

A written text will feel more 'conversational' if it has at least some of these features:

- ▶ A sense of you, the reader, being present, even if you're not:
    - ❏ *Direct forms* of address ('we' and 'you') and presence of the actors; the avoidance of passives.
    - ❏ *'Interactive' forms*, such as questions and FAQs (which imply the presence of a listener/reader).
    - ❏ *Conversational asides or fillers* (in fact, of course, mind you, since you asked).

- ▶ Some other features of spoken language may also be used within the written language in a dialogic or conversational discourse. Like this:
    - ❏ *Lack of 'polish'* – non-sentences and other things that can be considered 'errors' or improper grammar.
    - ❏ *The lexicon is simpler* – in English this would be drawn from older English rather than Latin/French-derived vocabulary.
    - ❏ *The construction is simpler* – clause length and sentence length are shorter, there's use of non-sentences, fewer complex sentences and fewer subordinate clauses.
    - ❏ *Using contractions* – as I've done here – and perhaps *colloquial* or everyday expressions.

An important effect of conversationality is to establish (or mimic) a more 'equal' relationship between the author of a text (or statement) with readers (or listeners). Conversation in real life characteristically entails a temporary suspension of existing status differences, far more than would ever be achieved in written language.

As I explained earlier, with the clear rise in use of the conversational mode in public and business discourse, including within governments and other serious institutions, monologic discourse is increasingly losing power and authority and is sounding stuffy, exclusive and dated.

Politeness and 'facework'

There are features of language known as 'politeness strategies' that do important social interactive work by reducing the effect of what are known as 'face-threatening acts'. Simply put, common face-threatening social actions are those that interfere with a person's sense of being respected, competent and approved of, and/or threaten their ability to do what they want. So simple everyday actions such as making a request, refusing a request or invitation, and offering an evaluation or challenge, even a minor one, are all 'face-threatening' to the other person.

In order to live relatively peacefully together, people and cultures everywhere develop shared social strategies for these situations: in British English, typically we mitigate the effect of these threats linguistically by 'facework', using 'politeness markers' like these:

- Polite terms/niceties (*please*).

- Hedging (*if possible, I wonder if, perhaps you would…*).

- Showing awareness of the imposition (*if it's okay with you*).

- Indirectness. A simple request might be expressed using language somewhere along this scale: '*Shut the window – Please shut the window – Could you shut the window please? – Shall we perhaps have the window shut now? – It's feeling a little cold in here.*' On this scale, the 'bald' instruction to 'shut the window' is the most face-threatening.

The important thing here is that the greater the power or status difference between participants, the less the need for 'face work' by the more powerful party. So, a parent might typically 'soften' a little, but not much, when making a request or denying their child something (face-threatening acts), because they have power and status advantages over the child. However, the same adult would be likely to mitigate requests and denials with politeness strategies when speaking with their boss or someone of high status. They'd also be likely do so with someone unknown to them, because to *not* mitigate face threats to a stranger can be understood socially as rude or even aggressive.

Why does this matter?

All of the above applies when people or groups within organizations are engaging with others and doing things such as:

▶ *Asking/telling others to do something* they might not want to do.

▶ *Preventing them* from doing something they *do* want to do.

▶ *Asking for something* from those others.

▶ *Giving feedback* or otherwise *commenting negatively* about aspects of them or their work.

These are, of course, very common acts for people in organizations of all kinds.

A routine failure to use appropriate politeness markers can be an assertion of superior status, because, from a position of power or higher status, we have less need to do so. We don't need to soften our requests or demands, there's less need to politely refuse what others demand of us, and less need to moderate our criticism of them, their ideas or their work. Therefore, the use or absence of politeness markers and face-saving language are clear indicators of perceived relative power. They offer rich information about the status that 'we' assume when engaging with 'them' – whether that 'we' is the team, the division, the subgroup or the whole organization.

There are, of course, internal local norms about politeness too. In some organizations or groups the norm is to be super-polite in every encounter (even if this masks something less civilized). In others this would be seen as pussyfooting and time-wasting, and 'bald' unmitigated requests, instructions or comments are the norm.

❖ What to look out for

We can look at an organization's language for markers of 'politeness' in this technical sense, or indeed the absence of them. We'd ask ourselves:

▶ Does language somewhere in the organization seem unusually blunt or brusque? What's it being used to do? Possible candidates would be:

☐ Exerting power? (You don't need to be polite if you're the one with power.)

☐ Is this an aspect of a pervasive parent-child dynamic?

☐ Is this brusqueness a way that organizational masculinity is being 'performed'? (Note: this language might actually be *used* by a man or woman but the same would apply.)

▶ Similarly, is there language that seems to be hyper-politeness, euphemism or pussyfooting? Again, what end is possibly being fulfilled by this?

☐ Avoidance of conflict? (May indicate that the potential for conflict is high.)

☐ Uncertainty about power/status within the relationship?

☐ Deference across a significant power/status gap?

☐ Contempt? (Being strenuously hidden.)

Note that there would be many *other* valid interpretations of such language – as always, it would need to be considered as part of a *pattern*, along with other clues picked up in other forms, to draw any useful inference from it.

In our consulting work, politeness and facework have sometimes proved useful in understanding cultural issues, as the following examples show:

Example 26: Open conflict

At a public sector organization where two professions were in deep conflict, in a few extreme cases we saw open 'rudeness' – for example, the total absence of the 'facework' that would have been appropriate in a particular meeting or exchange. A senior newcomer to the organization in fact expressed shock at witnessing one such exchange, because the social breach was so evident.

Example 27: Constrained by politeness

A men's health charity had an unspoken but lived 'rule' against offending anyone outside its walls. This showed clearly one day in their reactions to a government decision refusing to make a new drug available to 'their' men. We saw unbridled, angry language used in conversations internally, while heavily mitigated statements were made in public. People at the charity were *furious* internally, but their press release was polite and restrained, expressing only 'disappointment' in the decision. In context, this could have been much more strongly worded, while remaining within the bounds of appropriate politeness, but the cultural imperative not to offend held any outward expression of anger in check.

Example 28: Keeping the lid on a tense situation

We carried out a project with a healthcare provider at a time of great stress and difficulty within the healthcare system in the UK. The organization's leadership had asked us to help understand the cultural implications of the partnership working that they were engaged in.

For one part of the brief, we analysed exchanges between some of the client organization's people and their counterparts in partner organizations, alongside the conversations about the situation they had with our researchers.

Behind the scenes, people were using startlingly different language *about* partner agencies than when engaged *with* them in calls, meetings and in exchanges of email and documents. It's not unusual, of course, to see differences between these two kinds of interactions – backstage/frontstage – but it was noticeable how extreme both discourses were and how wide the gap was between them.

Behind the scenes

In the privacy of their own organization, and in backstage conversation with the researchers, people could use emotionally intensified language, and saw no need to hedge or pull back their comments. They used blunt and forthright, unmuted language, when frustration and unmitigated criticism broke through:

- 'It's catastrophic.'
- 'Really frustrating.'
- 'I hate it when they say that.'
- 'The relationships are not working. Absolutely not.'
- 'We have a crisis.'
- 'I'm thinking: oh for god's sake, here we go again.'
- 'There are days I get really cross.'

Interactions with partner agencies

In contrast, many of the organization's exchanges with partner agencies, in emails and meetings, were almost unnaturally hyper-polite. When dealing with partner agencies, they employed what we came to call a language of 'interactional caution.' Interactive care was being taken, at a level that in our experience is very unusual. There was much hedging, softening and use of politeness strategies around requests, and especially when giving any negative feedback. There was also a noticeable level of affiliative or 'stroking' language: language designed to foster, or express, a desire to create emotional bonds – a lot of thanking, complimenting, praising, informal greetings and friendly, 'personal' language:

- 'I hope you are feeling better and thanks for reading the slides so promptly.'
- 'That would be wonderful.'
- 'So, if you have time, your support will be most appreciated.'
- '... they've kindly investigated.'

- ▷ 'I need a little favour please.'

- ▷ '... some feelings of dissatisfaction.'

- ▷ 'If I could suggest that I think we perhaps could have had more of an update.'

- ▷ 'I do wonder, I suppose, if that will address the issues.'

It appeared that politeness strategies were being used to keep the lid on a very difficult and tense situation. The politeness work was necessary, and was generally working to preserve the service, but it was taking a great deal of emotional labour to maintain and could not be sustained.

So, we have now completed the three parts of the 'culture pie' and addressed the last of my three big culture questions. In this chapter, about organizational habits concerning relationships, we've focused on what language can tell us about issues of power, and about related elements within how relationships operate, including how we signal distance/closeness, linguistic markers of class and education, and cultural conventions about politeness.

———

In the chapters of this section, we've gone through a lot of detail and examples of language features and patterns that are useful in analysing organizational culture. It's now time to consider what comes next – making sense of those features and patterns, and using that insight to do useful cultural work.

SECTION III:

HOW WE CHANGE THINGS AROUND HERE

This final section outlines the approach we developed at Linguistic Landscapes to help clients work with the outcomes of the cultural discourse analyses I've just described. Doing so means collating and sharing insights and working with teams to devise simple principles to help a transition towards a revised set of cultural assumptions, if that's indeed what's required.

It also means finding ways to keep the insight alive; this isn't a one-off analysis and enforced change, but a process of raising cultural awareness for everyone. That way it remains easier to see the contribution of culture and to optimize it for current and as yet unseen needs.

Chapter 8
Pulling the analysis together

Language patterns, as I've explained, can strongly suggest the important dimensions and characteristics of an organizational culture. This analysis won't define what it *is* but can point to potential unspoken assumptions and unwritten norms and invite those involved to consider those.

How true do they feel to people's lived experience of working within the organization? And what implications flow from those insights?

The significance of qualitative analysis

So far in our own consulting work we've done this work largely qualitatively – that is, through disciplined data gathering and analysis and informed interpretation of unstructured material such as language. I need to stress that the methods I describe are *research* – qualitative research. Free-form language is rich in meaning, but qualitative analysis does need to be anchored in a *systematic* reading of *enough* data.

It's beyond my scope here to go into details about the full qualitative analytic process, but there are many books on this, including my own (Ereaut 2002). Interpretative qualitative research can provide rich insight but must be grounded in data if it's to be useful (in the same way that numbers without meaningful interpretations are just numbers).

In particular, one or two data points – snippets of language – do not make an analysis: we're looking for *patterns*. (Please note again that I've used single examples of language throughout this book to illustrate a point or set of findings, but these have all been chosen to be examples of the wider patterns and their aggregation from which we drew conclusions.)

Like a jigsaw puzzle, the analyst collects pieces that seem to have some similarity, then sees if and how they fit together. Unlike a puzzle, we rarely have the full set of pieces, nor a picture on the box to guide us, but when you see an image emerging, you see it!

Example 29: Finding a 'parent-child' relationship norm

A cultural dimension needs to show up in several language patterns across a range of language data to be worth bringing back for consideration by the organization.

I mentioned earlier an organization with what looked like an all-pervasive 'parent-child' relationship norm. In analysis, this was read from multiple language examples and features, including: the dominance of deontic modalities in everyday conversation, documents and email (*ought, should, must* verb forms); the common use of abrupt, unhedged monologic language, especially in emails; and multiple examples of public 'bossing' language, including notices about washing-up, storing food, etc. in the shared kitchens. These notices were often produced in duplicate or triplicate, in capitals, stuck to the walls – they almost seemed to be shouted.

Showing examples of this pattern to a wide range of people within the organization, with multiple examples gathered on one slide, produced laughter and exclamations of recognition. However – and this is its value – those responses also provoked consideration and widespread conversations over a long period about the 'parent-child' issue.

Crucially, this cultural tendency couldn't be attributed to one person or set of leaders – it was clear that almost everyone had become implicated in enacting and unconsciously replicating it.

People commissioning such work sometimes become concerned about the validity of interpretation in qualitative research – how can we know that it's showing something that's *real*? In fact, we've found that the harshest and thus most persuasive test of validity for an analysis of culture via language is to share it widely with those inside the organization. By that I mean at least several presentations given to a hundred or more people at a time, drawn from across divisions and grades. If we've touched into the roots of a relevant organizational culture (and perhaps shone light on felt, but as yet unspoken, tensions or struggles), there will be:

▷ A clear recognition of the patterns – most typically people say, 'That makes complete sense and feels really familiar, but I never saw it before.'

▷ Immediate offers of fresh examples of language or actions that fit the patterns.

▷ A degree of astonishment and wonder, and sometimes laughter, as people suddenly see something that's so familiar to them – their own shared language – in a completely different light. This often releases a burst of energy, and is 'insight' in a true sense of the word.

There's more on the significance of sharing analysis findings in Chapter 9.

Making the implicit explicit – no matter what it is

At this later stage of analysis, we look first for any apparent 'truths' that, no matter how unexpected, the organization's language keeps pointing to. What deep assumptions seem to be made, and might any of these be limiting? Those apparent 'truths' often concern questions of core identity – who we *really* are, and what will *always* matter around here. For example, is there an obsession with regulation and control? Or with our own heroic story? Or a deep avoidance of conflict? Making these explicit as working hypotheses, no matter what they are, is important and useful.

❖ Why this matters

Why might it matter, or help, to make unspoken and possibly embarrassing 'truths' explicit?

▷ It's very hard for people internally to *see* them – and thus to see them as having any alternative.

▶ They're the essence or identity of the place – often rooted back in the mists of time.

▶ They're deeply held and felt, even if unconsciously – 'we shall defend these truths to the death.'

These shared but unspoken beliefs give a strong sense of belonging, loyalty and engagement, but can also prove to be beliefs that have become limiting because the external context and/or internal priorities have changed. Such beliefs are *impossible* to shift if not recognized and discussed, at least as a first step.

❖ What to look out for

There may be core ideas that are unlikely to be spoken out loud but that are the inevitable higher-level conclusion from a long period of observation, or across a large collection of data.

▶ We'd normally write out our first thoughts about an organization's or group's core assumptions like this: WE BELIEVE... WE ASSUME... THIS IS TRUE... At this point, too, it's worth spelling out what the limitations (or indeed untapped potential) might be of each core assumption.

Even if what emerges at this point is surprising or unpalatable, listing out those things that seem to be leaking into language and that on examination may be plausible, is a valuable way to bring the analysis together.

Here are a few examples to show what I mean, along with a version of the limitation we identified along with the client at the time:

▶ **We are honourable and noble** – limiting because the market means we're having to shift to less pure and 'worthy' products.

▶ **We are the small group of brave ones who will change the world** – limiting because supporters now want to be included and involved, not to be made to look on and feel grateful.

▶ **We are on the side of truth and morality** – limiting because an absolutist moral position is now an expensive aim, and we have to embrace pragmatism.

▷ **We are the biggest and best; we don't need anything from anyone else** – limiting because working with partners is now the only way we can survive, and they also have some good ideas.

▷ **We are a movement, the very opposite of a business** – limiting because we absolutely have to make money if the movement is to continue.

▷ **We are amazing/at our best in a crisis (and actually we love them)** – limiting because crises are inefficient, even solved ones, and we need to organize better to avoid them.

▷ **That's just how we *are* around here** – limiting because 'just how we are' simply won't cut it anymore – the world has moved on and is leaving us behind.

Beyond these big ideas, we also aim to identify the other silent assumptions evident in language that might be less all-encompassing but that underpin observable behaviour and choices, or indeed problems and conflict. Attempting to specifically answer the three questions in the culture 'pie' will probably throw up some more assumptions to add to the list.

Again, here are our early version answers from two past projects to make this clearer:

Example 30: Potential answers to a UK public authority's culture questions

---

Who are we and what matters here?

▷ We're the biggest and best, the leaders in our field.

▷ Nothing here will ever change. New leaders come and go, and they make a bit of noise, but this too shall pass.

▷ We're individually safest in our small groups, in our caves.

▷ If in doubt, keep your head down, don't look up.

▷ Keep everything, never throw it away, because you might need it when the next regime arrives.

Who do we think 'they' are outside, and what do we think of them?

- Partner agencies are inferior to us.
- Other public authorities are inferior to us.
- Citizens/residents – who?

How do we do relationships around here?

- Hierarchy is all-important so never speak out of turn and you'd better jump when someone important tells you to.
- We're especially scared of one particular 'high-up' group, so avoid contact so they don't ask questions.
- Friendliness is dangerous and unnecessary outside your own 'cave', so don't do it.
- Everyone here will behave like a child unless you tell them not to/I want to be told what to do and not take responsibility.
- Because partner agencies are inferior, we need to take charge.

Example 31: Potential answers to a men's health charity's culture questions

Who are we and what matters here?

- Nice people.
- Mild and polite.
- A little embarrassed at the delicacy of our subject.
- Furious in private about the injustice involved.
- We must be seen to be scientific and objective.

Who do we think 'they' are outside, and what do we think of them?

- Men with this illness and their families are to be pitied and helped.

- The medical profession and scientists/researchers are to be held in awe and kept happy.

- Members of Parliament must be respected, flattered and cajoled.

How do we do relationships around here?

- We must never offend anyone.

- Not saying what we really think, not making waves.

- Even if angry, we stay super-polite.

- Using euphemisms to avoid offending.

Here's one last set of examples, drawn from three different consulting projects that focused on the question: who are 'they' out there? These examples of core assumptions are less about core identity, but were unspoken, deeply held beliefs about what was *outside*, and that were, as before, ultimately limiting and dysfunctional, given each organization's context and strategy (these limitations are added in brackets):

- **Our customers, unfortunately, are rather stupid. Not our problem; it's just the way it is**. (Our competitors are dealing with the same customers: they don't look down on them and are making it easier for them. And we're losing business because of this.)

- **If customers don't like us, that's their failing and their fault. If they bothered to get to know us, they'd love us.** (They have no obligation to bother with us. If we want their business, we have to make it easy for them to know and love us.)

- **Our customers need us more than we need them.** (No, they really don't. They'll find a way to leave if they can.)

Working with the client team and a broader group of staff and managers, at this point we'd start to ask whether the culture that emerges is serving the organization or group well. Consider the findings in the light of the organization's current situation and strategy:

- What in the cultural profile remains essential and positive – and could even be amplified?

▶ What if anything could benefit from being challenged or evolved? What's now potentially problematic for the business or organization?

▶ What other implications or effects are there that might be a result of this culture leaking out beyond the organization's doors? For example, does it colour relationships with partners and with customers/users, or has it interfered with past attempts to change?

Our experience suggests that doing preliminary thinking about these ourselves as external consultants is valuable, but the power comes when larger numbers of people from right across the organization can come to this understanding themselves. So we develop a possible cultural story or profile and take people through it, showing the patterns in everyday language and the meanings that seem to us to flow from them. The crucial test is whether people recognize this picture and that it's coherent. This gives people at all levels back some conscious choice – is this cultural trait helpful to us anymore? If not, what can we do differently? In this way, together, numerous groups can work towards necessary actions.

Chapter 9
Working with what emerges

First, let's revisit what this kind of cultural analysis is *for* and how could one apply it. This book has largely been about a diagnostic approach to surfacing important but implicit assumptions within a given organization culture. Processes for *using* what emerges will necessarily vary greatly according to the organizational objectives being addressed (see the Introduction for some examples of these).

However, I believe that all action in relation to culture has to start with a clear, non-judgemental but unflinching description of the current state of affairs – the 'as is' – and an exploration of its implications.

The first step (after the analysis has been shared with the immediate commissioning team) is sharing and exploring the emerging patterns and insights with others in the organization, including but not limited to its leadership.

The second step is creating a simple aide-memoire based on the analysis, to anchor the shared insight and the sense of what's needed – we usually call these 'working principles'. Let's look at what's involved in each of those two steps.

Sharing insights – the 'aha' moment and the 'oh dear' moment

Culture is replicated everywhere, so changing a specific system, or executing a reorganization, or making an announcement, won't change the habits of culture. (It's like moving to a new house and expecting your family suddenly to be tidy and stop fighting over washing the dishes.) To change, one needs coordinated, collective understanding, commitment and effort – and this has to start with a widespread shared awareness of how things are *now*.

After the analysis, we share findings extensively in large mixed-level groups. By that I mean several presentation and discussion sessions, ideally given in person to a hundred or more people at a time, who have been drawn from across divisions and grades. Remote working has, of course, changed the viability of this, but it's still the gold standard; there's something about people discovering new insights *together* in person and in large groups that sparks some kind of continuing large-scale conversation, and in this there can be the beginnings of real change.

There are a few things that are vital to how these findings should best be shared:

> It must be made clear that no one is being blamed, or held to be at fault, even if the cultural assumptions that emerge are recognized as outdated or difficult in some other way. We normally remind the audience about the 'first day at work' story – everyone acquired these cultural norms when they were new and were in no position to comment. In addition, old patterns are based in past adaptive cultures. Implicit norms may look negative or unhelpful now but, in our experience, dysfunctional patterns in culture can always be traced back to a time when they made perfect sense for the organization and for the conditions at the time. It's important not to judge specific people or groups, nor to allow this to happen. An overtly non-judgemental and empathetic approach is important – it doesn't just make these findings acceptable but allows them to be powerful in changing how people can think about their organization.

> Sharing the *evidence* is important too – showing illustrations of the language patterns. People at all levels respond well to analysis

that's evidence-based, well-illustrated and accessible, and not opaque or baffling.

▶ People will, of course, need to know that senior leadership has seen the analysis and is behind this. In fact, it's better if they're also in the room or meeting and can be seen to be absorbing the analysis and seeing people's reaction along with everyone else. This helps acceptance and engagement across levels. It takes a level of courage for leadership to face up in public to the reality of culture – not to point fingers or offer defensiveness, but to accept collectively the way things are, even if they then wish to encourage change.

There are two key questions for this meeting, and for immediately after it:

Q 1. Do you recognize this picture of us and how we are?

People generally respond with their gut over their brain: visceral recognition vs cognitive understanding – and this is powerful.

Illustrated findings lead to a moment of insight: 'I totally recognize that but have never seen it before' – this is energizing and intriguing. There's often laughter as people suddenly see their own familiar language and world differently.

This shock of recognition is what we've come to call the 'aha' moment. What happens at this point may then feel like relief – whatever is lurking underneath is now out in the open and can be discussed, and current struggles may make more sense. We often observe a release of energy; a few people will immediately see the insight as liberating them from old habits and unwritten rules, while others are excited and curious but sceptical.

People will often then add examples or build on the insight. And occasionally someone will offer a thought on where something originally came from – perhaps some forgotten incident, or an influential person in the past. The history is long gone, but the legacy remains. Such explanations or theories are interesting if they arise but are not necessary to this process.

However, the 'aha' is swiftly and necessarily followed by a related moment – possibly an 'oh dear' one – as people consider how far the current culture is or is not helping them. The next collective question is:

Q2: How far is this set of assumptions – our cultural unspokens – helpful to us now?

What if anything needs to change for our organization to thrive today? Where and how do our shared habits of thinking and acting now need conscious rework? What should we amplify, amend, or lose?

One client recently described the 'aha' and the 'oh dear' moments this way:

> 'When presenting their [long] presentation to groups of hundreds of staff... [the agency] got a profound reaction. Scales fell from eyes. Staff were recognizing the unseen, unheard conventions.
>
> Staff were laughing at the familiarity of what they had experienced but hadn't labelled or consciously been aware of. They were also shocked at the harm that some of it caused – especially [one cultural habit] – to individuals and teams, services and users.'

It can be helpful to divide cultural norms and assumptions into simple categories, thus highlighting the likely attention that they'd need to support the overall culture:

▶ 'Burdens' (aspects of culture that are now a liability) – 'release and remove.'

▶ 'Sparks' (aspects of the culture that would warrant nurturing) – 'amplify and encourage.'

▶ 'Gaps' (missing elements that could be beneficial to the overall culture, such as curiosity about the world outside the organization) – 'inspire action to fill.'

Some people change immediately – quite literally they start having different conversations. Others need more help to hang on to the insight and the possibilities it offers. Either way, it's important to do *something* immediately at this point while the insight is still visceral and the internal conversation is bubbling.

What seems to be going on in this process? Developing the model I introduced in Chapter 3, we can think of this activity as helping people in the organization to consider shifting their current 'silent assumptions' to bring them closer to serving the current strategy and aims of the organization:

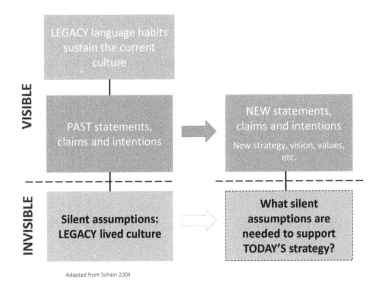

Adapted from Schein 2004

The first stage is to bring the existing cultural norms to awareness in the form of the analysis and its answers to the three culture questions. There should then be debate about how useful those cultural norms are, allowing a combination of researchers and members of the organization to sketch out an alternative set of unspoken assumptions (which will, of course, *not* be unspoken, at least at first). Capturing these in the form of working principles – see next section – gives both a reminder of the current thinking and interaction, and a 'scaffolding' to help people evolve new cultural habits:

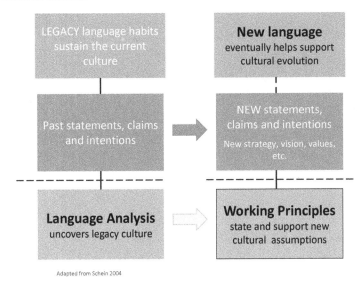

Adapted from Schein 2004

Working principles

Over the years that we've used this research approach, we've developed some simple tools for taking cultural insight forward. After sharing and refining ideas about the unspoken culture, we can then help people in the organization ask: what would our silent assumptions need to be *now* in order to help us achieve our current aims?

This leads to a tailored approach to 'how we could do it differently', and simple 'working principles' to anchor this insight and intent, keep it visible and help to course-correct (or more radically challenge) cultural habits of thinking and acting. There are many different ways to think and talk about the things I'm referring to here as 'working principles', including:

> *A shared attitude*

> *A way of being*

> *A mindset*

> *A north star*

> *An ethos*

> *A reminder of how we're trying to be*

> *Commitments*

> *Touchstones*

> *How we do things around here*

One of these terms or ideas may make most sense to an organization or team when developing and discussing them, or a new one may be invented – one client called theirs the 'Words Matter Principles'. Principles can be deceptively simple statements, such as **'Be honest and unembarrassed'** or **'Assume good intent in others'**. However, because they've sprung from and are tied to the analysis that made cultural issues obvious to all, they're robust and powerful for guiding conversations and activities.

Note that these principles are not intended to replace or compete with other high-level documents such as mission, vision and values statements, although one of our client organizations did adopt them to replace a values statement. Instead, they're best thought of as a temporarily spoken set of 'unspokens', used to hold the insight in place and keep it visible to everyone while the efforts to change multiple expressions of culture can be made.

It's important that such principles are simple, active, action-oriented statements, and not abstract nouns or verbs. One of the problems with many organizations' public claims about 'our culture' or statements of values is that they tend to be highly abstract and compressed terms ('excellence' or 'caring'). With these, it can be impossible for staff to see how to apply them to their everyday work.

Simple clean principles, each with a clear explanation based in the analytic insight, create a scaffolding to help foster a change in conversations and actions. Experience from many engagements shows us that in drafting useful working principles, we need to:

- Focus on those cultural dimensions: a) that are important to the organization's or group's objectives; and b) where current norms are unhelpful or even toxic.

- Use principles to be clear about how everyone in the organization needs to aim to 'be' culturally.

- Use simple imperatives – be, do, understand, remember, think, make. Principles need to be expressed in a clear and helpful way, not in a punitive or aggressive one. They must be a catalyst for conversations about how to do things, not a draconian set of orders.

- Limit them to a maximum of about five – this seems to work best.

- Avoid cliches and generics – principles must be specific to the organization, and specific to its situation *now*.

- Link back to the cultural insight work and why each particular principle is needed.

- Make each one distinct from the others.

- Indicate their potential use beyond language.

- Add examples and illustrations.

We've found it helpful to organizations if we create a preliminary prototype set of principles that flow logically from the analysis, in the context of the organizational need that prompted the work in the first place. However, they're infinitely stronger once refined by sets of people from across the organization in informal discussion workshops, before being finalized and captured as a working document and perhaps memorable graphic of some kind.

Ultimately these principles could again become unspoken – just 'the way we do things around here' – but they need to be conscious and visible for long enough for new habits to form and different interactions to become normalized. They're like signposts at the edge of an established path, encouraging people to strike out across the long grass to form new paths; eventually the 'new paths' just become 'the paths' and are obvious to everyone.

Ideally, principles influence small but coordinated changes – in micro-decisions, in how people interact, in how priorities are set. Cultural change at scale takes a long time, as everyone agrees, and these principles are best used in everyday work, in teams or groups where they can have small almost immediate effects, rather than being published as 'top-down' orders.

They generally have a long life and are not one-off items for an immediate fix; clients use them in many ways to reflect on, check in on and work on evolving their cultures through periods of change, and they may be updated and revised as progress is made.

You might notice I've used terms such as 'evolve' for what happens to the culture. 'Culture change' to my ear implies overthrowing and replacing it, and I dislike the implications for staff (and indeed managers) of the idea that change is *made* to happen in one action or finite programme of work, especially via the ubiquitous idea of 'levers'. Evidence suggests that, despite its dominance, the model of an organization as a machine, where certain high-level actions have predictable outcomes, is not the most useful. People are not cogs in a perfect machine (or even an imperfect one) – they're human, with all the complexity and potential for inventiveness and change that entails.

With human relationships and emotions involved, the model of an organization as a complex set of interactions and processes appears to be a far more accurate and useful one. So helping people to 'evolve' or 'adapt' their collective assumptions can acknowledge and respect cultures as rooted in human psychology and relationships, and makes it clear too that they're dynamic. A static or unchanging culture is where patterns of interaction and action are stuck in more or less repeating loops. To allow adaptation to new conditions, this stable state needs help to shift, and this is a lot easier if the patterns and loops can be seen and recognized by those involved.

I see the analytic work I'm describing as giving feedback into the cultural system itself. That is, giving non-judgemental feedback on the nature of its invisible connectors (shared norms and assumptions) and how those are being held in place, and encouraging people to start to reconfigure the connectors, allows different behaviour to emerge. This may not happen all at once, but team by team, or event by event, or site by site, it's a real possibility.

Each principle is unpacked by a simple one-page 'what this is and why we need it' and together these simple items form the basis for a range of activities – see Chapter 10.

As an example, here are three from a set of five principles produced to address internal cultural conflict that was hampering the work and development of a particular business:

> **Assume good intent and recognize everyone's value**

> **Value continuity as well as change**

> **Listen respectfully, explain politely**

You might look at these principles and think, well, that's obvious – these are simply the principles of good and healthy behaviour among colleagues inside an organization. That's true, but only up to a point. The analysis of this organization's language showed norms and indeed some behaviour that *wasn't* good and healthy, hence the need to state these things explicitly. Others are far more specific to hotspots in the organization. All principles must fall directly out of the analysis, as this is an important way that they're real and meaningful for staff. But we often find that principles are of two kinds:

> *Hygiene principles*: these state behaviour that would be widely regarded as best practice, but that's simply not in place in the organization. They might include principles of interactive behaviour, as above, or principles of good contemporary customer communications.

▶ *Remedial principles*: these address head-on the issues that are specific to that organization and that emerge from the analysis as being important to current problems and therefore in need of work. Unsurprisingly, sometimes these are resisted by senior leadership – what leader would want, for example, '**Don't create fear in others**' or '**Be honest**' to require public statement? (Both of these are real examples.) However, they're generally accepted in the end, as the demonstrated need for them across the community of the organization becomes acknowledged and outweighs the senior-level discomfort.

Example 32: Getting closer to customers

A division of a large US firm was eager to sell its services to owners of small businesses. As part of a huge corporate, team members within this division felt they knew what those business owners needed, and this tended to result in slightly boastful and monologic communication, which also used 'corporate' business language.

The client's team's own internal discourse was also inclined to subtly position the business owner as a little inept and struggling; that is, desperately in need of the company's help. None of this was helping them make good emotional connections with this target market, where resilience and self-sufficiency are points of pride.

Again, here are three principles from the total set of five:

▶ **Be humble**: remember they're doing pretty well without us.

▶ **Remember they're in charge**: they're competent people making their own decisions.

▶ **Think like a customer, talk like a customer**: use their language, not ours.

In this case, the first two were 'remedial' principles for them, and the last one a 'hygiene' principle.

'Working principles', not 'language principles'

Just because we've used language as a way *in* to a culture, it doesn't mean that language is the only way *out*, nor the best way to encourage change in organizational culture – quite the opposite, in fact. You can't change culture by mandating a change in language, nor by fixing internal or external 'communications' alone – attempts at this are likely to be dismissed as trivial or resisted as the work of 'the language police'.

However, I've argued throughout this book that language has a key role in organizations as it both reflects and reproduces an organization's 'deep' culture, and language is one instrument to help challenge and shift it. It's most important that people in the organization see what their language is *doing* – the unconscious habits of thinking and interacting that are being reflected and held in place by existing language habits – and are then encouraged to try a range of things to change those habits.

For internal reasons our analysis outputs have sometimes been launched internally by a client as 'language principles', even when intervening in the culture was the aim. Within a particular organizational context this has been done tactically, to legitimize and help them to be spread and used immediately. Very often, though, people quickly realize that they're *cultural* principles and that they can and should affect every action that people take, from the big strategic decisions to the tiniest micro-decisions made by an individual at their desk. If and how they're then 'outed' as *cultural* principles is an internal matter of politics and influence.

Working principles that end up labelled as 'language principles' can certainly help improve external and internal communications, but they're *not* 'tone of voice' documents or communications guidance. The difference is that analysis-based and culturally informed 'language principles' connect communications language back into the deep culture of the organization. They work to stem or amend the flow of attitudes and habits from inside the culture that may have been problematic in connecting with customers or with staff, tackling the problem at root. If they become separated from the internal cultural insights that led to them, they're at the mercy of the gravitational pull of the existing familiar culture and language, and communications are likely to slide back into supporting that culture.

Chapter 10
Into the future: a cultural
health plan

Keeping the culture conversation going

Once an organization has done the immediate analysis work on language and discourse, people may well generate other initiatives and/or start to incorporate that work into ongoing initiatives in the organization. If we think of organizational culture as located within ongoing everyday interactions, and in their consequences such as decisions, it's helpful to use cultural analysis work to establish and sustain a kind of 'culture conversation' across the organization. That is, making culture both a topic of normal conversation and also helping people realize that every conversation and action is cultural. (By 'conversations', I'd include the implicit ones people have with themselves in their minds as they made decisions, take actions, choose between alternatives and so on.) That is, culture can be regarded as important, wide-ranging and essentially alive – an ongoing process to be engaged with positively, not just when there seems to be a problem.

There isn't a standard or prescribed process for this, because every organization must work with its unique cultural fingerprint and address its own organizational needs. However, here are a few general comments on how we've seen this process unfold.

Working with working principles

Typically, clients will first go on to derive other practical tools from the core set of working principles, often with our help. We've seen all of these be successful in different contexts:

- ▶ 'The Book' – simple, illustrated explanation and guidance for all staff on the outcomes of the analysis and the principles, including why they're needed and how they work.

- ▶ Workshops to develop applications, tailored to specific groups (e.g. a workshop on 'difficult customer conversations', or to work through an identified internal impasse).

- ▶ Visible reminders of the principles – posters, screensavers, desk reminders, intranet pages, microsite, etc. These should be relatively simple and low-key, and not look like a shiny, expensive 'change initiative'. Such visible items don't *do* the work but serve to remind people of the ideas behind the principles, and to help them make different choices, one conversation or micro-decision at a time.

- ▶ Creating 'demonstrators' or before-and-after documents showing how the organization or team *sounds* different when speaking from a different set of unspoken assumptions. These allow people to feel for themselves the way in which different attitudes and relationships are beamed out or constructed by different language. Again, all this applies to spoken as well as written language, internal and external, formal and informal.

- ▶ Including some high-visibility and high-importance items – they let people see that the organizational leadership is committed to the process.

It's important that individuals, managers and teams also apply principles well beyond language – to decisions, processes, priorities and more. Ideally, working principles will be integrated into ongoing activities and processes, and especially to high-visibility and/or wide-reach projects or items. Preferably, leaders and managers would be constantly referencing them in meetings; and they would feature within formal and informal reviews and conversations – essentially weaving them into the fabric of the organization's everyday life.

I've sometimes suggested that people involved in this work create an organizational 'acupuncture map' – identifying the points and moments in the organization (perhaps people, teams, products, initiatives, etc.) where focusing effort on this would bring disproportionate effect.

Beware the shadow side

One point about ongoing use of principles: it's worth being aware of the 'shadow side' of each principle; that is, any positive principle, taken to extremes, can become counterproductive. For example, 'be honest and unembarrassed' has a shadow that's something like 'be hurtful, be brutal and embarrass others'.

It's also worth monitoring 'cherry-picking', where an individual or group attempts to defend unhelpful behaviours by the selective application of just one of the principles. So riding roughshod over others might be defended as being in line with the principle to 'be bold and energetic', without consideration for one or more of the others – such as 'be responsive and supportive'. We usually emphasize that there's a certain minimum level for all principles, and that they're joined together as a linked set of ideas.

Ongoing training, showing examples and reminding people about why the principles are there, and the good work they can do, is entirely possible and is effective to address both these issues.

When startups grow up

In most of this book I've been focusing on analysis as problem diagnosis – the uncovering of cultural issues that potentially underpin known or suspected organizational problems. Typically, organizations only seek answers, and therefore spend money on research and consultants, when they have an issue that they don't think they can solve themselves.

Requests for a different application of this method do sometimes arise though, and we've also helped young and growing organizations to support existing success and further growth. Here I'll outline two examples of what happens when, rather than a remedial process of working on gaps, our task has been to perform a health check on a positive but fast-growing organization culture, to *keep it on track* and *develop its cultural assets* as it grows.

When an organization is new and small, and especially when led by people who care about the idea of culture, it often has a thriving and coherent culture that's perfectly adapted to its situation and environment, heavily influenced by its founders or leaders. 'Our culture' may well be a frequent and easy topic of conversation, and indeed a topic for celebration – it makes everyone feel good to be working in a culture that... well... *works*.

However, the environment and situation for which the culture is perfect are definitely going to change, because the organization will grow, perhaps take on new areas of work, and/or its operating conditions will change, and/or new people will arrive, at all levels. So even the 'perfect' culture is likely over time to be put under some strain.

The presenting issue here may be expressed as, 'We have a fabulous culture; how can we hang on to it, even as we grow?' We'd encourage that client to reframe this question – it's not just about how to *hang on* to a great culture but also how to gently *evolve* it. What makes a culture fantastic for a small fast-growing startup may not be what will get it successfully and happily through the next phases of its existence – perhaps a 'business as usual' or 'steady growth' period.

Example 33: Building on good foundations

The leaders of a small, successful and rapidly growing supplier of specialist B2B services were proud of their existing culture and saw it as essential to their early success. However, they noticed that the organizational culture had been changing over the past few years and that this was bringing challenges:

▶ As they grew, it had become harder to informally 'check in' with people, so the old certainty and confidence regarding the culture – what it was like and why it worked – was no longer universal.

▶ In addition, regulatory pressure around their work had grown as they expanded, and the regulator now featured more prominently in their world – there was a new, demanding and powerful actor on their stage.

▶ For the first time, occasional customer-related challenges had emerged. This had rather shaken their view of customers as being wonderful and 'just like us'.

▶ These factors had also created the conditions for micro-cultures to begin to develop, with some negative effects, and the leadership team was keen to stop this progressing.

They knew that the culture that had made them successful in the first few years may not be the same culture they needed for continued success and growth. So our analysis focused on showing what they already had to build on, and suggesting what building on it might look like.

They'd described their culture as 'innate' – but sensitive codification of that 'innateness' allowed them to understand what they already had, in a way that made it accessible to discussion, debate and conscious choice. A common language for the current culture came from the analysis; a common language for their future culture came from working through the analysis with the senior team and co-creating a set of tailored principles.

Example 34: Starting out and keeping going with cultural intent

A good example of using linguistic analysis right at the outset in the creation of a new organization was a public sector/government body that was in the process of forming a brand-new set of services and breaking away from its parent organization. When we first met its leadership, it was not yet a legal entity.

▶ The CEO designate was determined that the culture of the new organization should be quite different from that of the parent organization (and indeed from the culture typical of other organizations in that sector) and had a clear vision for it. His personal influence and charisma were highly influential in the early days as they recruited a team to build the new organization.

▶ However, as in the previous example, this CEO was aware that the culture that had made them successful as they were in the exciting period of startup – energetic, inclusive and fun, with a 'teenage' optimism and energy – might need to evolve for continued success and growth.

▶ It was crucial to the new entity that it established a good working relationship with the 'parent' entity, so the two very different cultures also needed to find a way to be compatible.

▶ Initially we analysed both cultures, to help both organizations develop how they could best work together.

▶ Later, we revisited the new organization's culture on a couple more occasions. This continued feedback helped the leadership team steer a course that capitalized on the undoubted assets within the culture (as an indicator, staff engagement scores were exceptionally high), while evolving it into a mature and functioning organization, ready for new ventures and growth.

Tracking progress

We recommend checking in on cultural evolution by reanalysing language at regular intervals – perhaps every two years or so. This could sound like a self-serving consultant's charter! However, following the initial analysis and its validation by the organization itself, keeping track is a far lighter-touch process – simply checking in on language samples and key items for obvious signs of progress, or of regression. This continues the process of giving feedback to people about their own collective behaviour and maintains awareness of culture.

Small or startup organizations are more likely to continue the 'culture conversation' easily, as culture is often seen as important enough to need investment and conscious nurturing early on. Leaders of established organizations, whose presenting problem was perhaps associated with a stagnant or toxic culture, will need to work harder to keep culture in the minds and discourse of people across the organization.

There's obvious difficulty in 'measuring' implicit human qualities such as unspoken assumptions and views of the world, and therefore in using numbers to assess progress made within a culture. In a numbers-driven, rationalized business and public environment, this poses a problem. I have no doubt, though, that the approach I've described here is effective, giving powerful feedback to those sharing a culture and allowing and encouraging them to reform their shared world for the better. This has proved to be an efficient and powerful method of cultural analysis and of engaging people in organizations in conversations about culture and change. Its outputs can be understood by people at all levels in organizations, from board to frontline, and it generates shared insight and language with which to encourage processes of change.

This approach to culture analysis is – pretty obviously – not at all like the large-scale quantified analyses of answers to survey questions, assessed against established norms and dimensions, that are commonly used in culture diagnosis. The linguistic analysis method I've described produces something different, and something that we observe brings many clients to a place of understanding about their culture that they've been struggling to achieve, and that they didn't know was possible. And it thus opens up different ways to think about intervening or helping to move the culture on, if that indeed is what's needed.

Significantly, our clients tell *stories* about the differences that they observe – progress may be irregular and not linear, but large and small wins are evident to them. One client reported it internally like this:

> 'Our change process was proving highly problematic, with potentially serious business consequences. We carried out linguistic analysis of senior and "official" discourse, and this pointed to systematic but unhelpful constructions of the change. Later work with staff fleshed out these insights and led to the creation of our [name] cultural principles. This resulted in an unblocking of key barriers at SLT/board level and significant improvements in staff survey results.'

Another senior leader we worked with addressed a conference of his peers this way:

> 'People – and organizational cultures – do not usually change because they are asked to do so, nor from the overwhelming strength of argument about the need to change (at least in the leaders' eyes), nor by the exhortation to "get on board". They change because they persuade themselves, often without realizing it. Rapport, listening, contributing and discussing and inviting people to elaborate can open a space for self-persuasion to happen – for most, if not all.

> *[We derived], with support, some "working principles". These are different from values. Action-oriented. Akin to the "simple rules" that govern the collective, coordinated movement of shoals of fish and flocks of birds. These working principles, allied with leadership and behaviours of the leader and chief executive, started having an effect, not just within the [organization's] culture, but also as the foundation of an employee value proposition for staff and how [the organization] was perceived externally.'*

If you're looking for analysis that peers deep into your culture at the level of human habit, emotion and belief – in all its messiness – and yet is supported by systematic and evidenced research, then this offers a tested and viable alternative.

Closing thoughts

In the Preface I set out my intention for this book: to share the learning that I and colleagues have acquired in developing this approach to organizational culture, and to invite you to consider how you could use this insight and experiment with the methods.

Practically speaking, you may feel you need to address your organization's culture right now, or to persuade others that it needs looking at. Perhaps you believe it isn't keeping pace with new strategies, new customer norms, new economic, market and social realities – or even that it has become in some way toxic.

It *is* possible to change culture – or at least create enough conversation to set it moving in a better direction – but you can't change something that you, and everyone working with you, can't see, understand or articulate. I do hope that the ideas and examples in this book will have given you some starting point for beginning to uncover it, as a critical step towards achieving what you need to do.

References

M. Bower, *The Will to Manage* (1966).

J. Butler, *Gender Trouble* (1990).

A. Cocks, *Counting the Dance Steps: Rethinking how we measure and change organisational cultures for the good of all* (2022).

T. Deal and A. Kennedy, *Corporate Cultures: The rites and rituals of corporate life* (1982).

G. Ereaut, *Analysis and Interpretation in Qualitative Market Research* (2002).

N. Fairclough, *Analysing Discourse: Textual analysis for social research* (2003).

V. Fournier, *Boundary Work and the (Un)Making of the Professions* (1999).

D. Grant and C. Oswick, *Metaphor and Organizations* (1996).

M. Jørgensen and L. Phillips, *Discourse Analysis as Theory and Method* (2002).

G. Lakoff and M. Johnson, *Metaphors We Live By* (1980).

G. Morgan, *Images of Organisation* (2006).

G. Morgan, https://academy.nobl.io/gareth-morgan-organizational-metaphors/

C. Mowles, *Complexity: A key idea for business and society* (2021).

J. Potter and M. Wetherell, *Discourse and Social Psychology: Beyond attitudes and behaviour* (1987).

C. Reynolds, 'Flocks, herds, and schools: a distributed behavioral model' in *Computer Graphics*, 21 (4), 25–34 (1987).

C. Rodgers, *Informal Coalitions: Mastering the hidden dynamics of organizational change* (2007).

C. Rodgers, *The Wiggly World of Organization: Muddling through with purpose, courage and skill* (2021).

E. Schein, *Organizational Culture and Leadership 3rd Edition* (2004).

P. Shaw, *Changing Conversations in Organisations: A complexity approach to change* (2002).

R. Stacey, *Complex Responsive Processes in Organizations: Learning and knowledge creation* (2001).

D. Sull, 'Why good companies go bad' in *Harvard Business Review*, 77 (4), 50–52, 183 (2005).

D. Tannen, *Gender and Discourse* (1996).

M. Weber, *Economy and Society* (1922).

Acknowledgements

Writing acknowledgements is a lovely part of creating a book, for the pleasure of publicly thanking those who have meant a great deal and added so much to one's working and personal life. However, it's also terrifying, for fear of omitting someone who should be named here. If I've done that, and it's you, I do hope that you'll forgive me.

Many thanks first to Kirstie Skates, for not only keeping the Linguistic Landscapes ship sailing since 2017 but tightening up the sails and plainly making the whole thing better. Huge thanks too to the marvellous Sara Smart, for a decade of support, sanity and serious fun from the earliest days of LL.

Sandra Pickering has offered me rock-solid support and benign challenge over several decades now, including provoking me into taking the business book proposal challenge that made this book happen. Thank you.

Thanks to Adam Morgan, for telling me about Edgar Schein's work and effectively changing my life. And I'm grateful to Edgar Schein himself for a challenging, stimulating and very useful conversation, sadly only days before he passed.

Thank you to Martin Fischer for an introduction to the world of complex adaptive systems, and for fun and learning as we worked out how to combine our approaches. I'm forever grateful to the late great Virginia Valentine of Semiotic Solutions, for demonstrating how to make social constructivism useful in the real world and for believing in my ability to develop my own version of it. Appreciation and respect go to the social science tutors at Goldsmiths, University of London, for taking me on as an

MA student at close to 40 years old and introducing me to the wonderful world of discourse analysis.

Many fantastic clients, colleagues and advisors have put their faith in me and this work and I want to thank them all (with special appreciation for the champions and early adopters, for sticking their necks out and giving it a go): they include Barb Agoglia, Janet Alexander, Dyfed Alsop, Alison Bain, Penny Ciniewicz, Michael Coughlin, Rachel Curtis, Debra Davies, Elliot Dunster, Moira Faul, Caroline Fawcett, Paul Feldwick, Vivienne Francis, Sarah Fryer, Richard Gilmore, Wendy Gordon, Katy Irving, Raymond Joabar, Clive Johnson, Jenni Lake, David Lowy, Dante Mastri, Alyson McGregor, Seamus O'Farrell, Mark Pearson, Karen Schannen, Randi Schochet, Jim Scopes, Jane Shirley, Susan Sobbott, Susan Stashower, Michael Szego, Judy Taylor, Mike Toms, Caroline Whitehill and Hilary Woods. Caroline Fawcett in particular has been a champion, advocate, serial client and all-round rock over many years and she has my heartfelt thanks.

I'm immensely grateful to Linguistic Landscapes' committed crew of analysts, researchers and collaborators who have contributed so much to the business, to the development of these ideas, and to me personally with their faith and enthusiasm as well as their skills: especially Clare Anderson, Simon Christmas, Louise Cretton, Mel Johnson, Veronika Koller, Emmet Ó Briain, Nat Segnit, Christine Shukis-Brown and Rebecca Whiting. Thanks too to past LL team members Kevin Cornwell, Oliver Daddow, Zsofia Demjen, Sally Hull, Marion Nao and Peter Turner.

Over the years Mark Stanton, Abi Searle-Jones and the whole crew at and/or/if LLP have dealt with our unreasonable information design requirements with skill and infinite patience – thank you. And thanks too to Nicki Brown at Transcribe It, for something very similar.

Several of those named above kindly read drafts of this book in an early form or discussed it with me and added immeasurably to it. Others who also helped in this way are Kathryn Bishop, Andrew Cocks, Chris Rodgers, Anza Tyrone and Duncan Wardley. All errors and omissions remain entirely mine, of course.

I want to thank Alison Jones for many things – for her remarkable business book proposal challenge, for awarding me a prize and a big vote of confidence, for her wise and inspiring coaching, for publishing this book – and for patience well beyond the call of duty. Thanks too to all the team at Practical Inspiration for flexibility and cheerfulness throughout, while Kathryn Bishop, Susan Ní Chríodáin and many other PIP authors generously shared their experiences and knowledge and offered emotional pit props when required – many thanks.

Lastly, huge personal thanks to my fabulous children, Joe Tanner and Millie Tanner, and to Nick Tanner, Nick Hicks and my extraordinary friends – for being around for me over the years, no matter how elusive or stressed or manic I became. Thank you.

Index

A quick word from Practical Inspiration Publishing...

We hope you found this book both practical and inspiring – that's what we aim for with every book we publish.

We publish titles on topics ranging from leadership, entrepreneurship, HR and marketing to self-development and wellbeing.

Find details of all our books at: www.practicalinspiration.com

 Did you know...

We can offer discounts on bulk sales of all our titles – ideal if you want to use them for training purposes, corporate giveaways or simply because you feel these ideas deserve to be shared with your network.

We can even produce bespoke versions of our books, for example with your organization's logo and/or a tailored foreword.

To discuss further, contact us on info@practicalinspiration.com.

 Got an idea for a business book?

We may be able to help. Find out more about publishing in partnership with us at: bit.ly/PIpublishing.

Follow us on social media...

 @PIPTalking

 @pip_talking

 @practicalinspiration

 @piptalking

 Practical Inspiration Publishing

Printed in the USA
CPSIA information can be obtained
at www.ICGtesting.com
JSHW062259221024
72178JS00010B/67